JASON HIMES

From Gangster To Reverend

A Journey Of Redemption

Contents

1

Introduction

This is a true narrative, but it isn't the type of story that usually associates with gang activity. Instead, this revolves around an adolescent Caucasian living in suburban America and his peers who have been ignored or cast aside by their families, teachers and caregivers. People often dismiss gangs comprised of white individuals as wannabes, but they originate from the same emotions of feeling lost and in need of somewhere to belong. Similarly to black and Mexican gangs at times portrayed on television or in movies, these white gangs can be just as big a problem for the towns they are settled into.

Jason was a product of his environment. Jason's early years were spent in a middle-class neighborhood, surrounded by the hum of lawnmowers and the laughter of children playing on manicured lawns. Raised by hardworking parents, his father spent nights on the job while his mother worked during the day. This left Jason to fend for himself before and after school as a latchkey kid.

As the younger sibling, he looked up to his older brother, Shawn, who was eight years his senior. Unfortunately for Jason, Shawn's life was a tumultuous one, constantly marred by trouble and poor decisions. This left an indelible impact on young Jason. When Jason began attending school, Shawn was no longer living with them. He had either been placed in a Juvenile facility or was staying with other family members.

Jason was an outcast, towering over the other kids but always too skinny. His clunky glasses made him a prime target of bullies throughout his school years. With his gangly frame and four-eyed look, Jason was labeled a nerd and geek by those around him.

Jason was frequently the target of bullying in his younger years, starting in kindergarten and throughout the next 8 years, he was chased, punched and kicked while the bullies laughed in his face. He never had any real friends, and this experience would haunt him for most of his teenage years. Through it all, he put on a mask of apathy but inside, he was always hurting and craving acceptance. His experiences with bullies would go on to form who he would become as an adult.

Freshman year of high school presented Jason with the opportunity to reinvent himself. He tossed his glasses and tried to befriend anyone who'd let him. The towering cafeteria buzzed with a variety of cliques: geeks, preppies, jocks, loners, and stoners. Jason gravitated towards the latter. Something about them sparked a thrill inside him and he quickly dove head first into their world. His "good boy" image began to crumble as time passed on.

At the age of 17, Jason was now working at the local arcade in a bustling city in Washington. With the arcade's neon lights filling up his world, he felt like he had finally found where he belonged: amongst the sounds of beeps and boops, and with kids who shared his passion for gaming. It was 1993, and the arcade was a bustling hub of excitement and energy, intermingled with the enthusiastic cries of patrons. The air was heavy with the scent of pizza and popcorn, creating an atmosphere that buzzed with life.

It was here that Jason first laid eyes on Ryan, John, Eric, and Tom. As different as they were from one another, they shared a bond that immediately caught Jason's attention.

Ryan, just 16, was scrawny and short, but his frame seemed to barely contain the frenetic energy that coursed through him. His intense demeanor hinted at a life fueled by drugs, yet beneath it all, there was a fierce loyalty that shone through. He was always ready for a fistfight and would defend his friends to the very end.

John, also 16, had the appearance of a country boy, with a rugged charm and a knack for mischief. He was a natural-born troublemaker, always on the lookout for easy money. His slightly crooked smile and mischievous eyes suggested a life of bending rules.

Eric, just 15, was John's younger brother and the tag-along of the group. With his scrawny frame and slightly awkward demeanor, he seemed to be living in his older brother's shadow. But there was a spark in his eyes that hinted at his own ambitions and desires.

Tom, the 17-year-old, stood out with his preppy style, his clean-cut appearance contrasting sharply with his surroundings. He carried himself with an air of confidence, a young man who knew what he wanted and would stop at nothing to get it.

As Jason observed them from a distance, he couldn't help but feel drawn to their tight-knit group and the sense of belonging they exuded. He found himself questioning whether he could ever fit in with them, torn between curiosity and the nagging feeling that he was stepping into dangerous territory. "Look at them," Jason thought, "they have each other's back no matter what."

Jason observed the group of teenage males, noticing that they were all wearing blue docker pants, plain white shirts, navy and white checkered fleece jackets and a blue bandana hanging out of their back pocket. As he had never encountered a gang before but had seen them on TV and in music, this sparked his interest. He was fascinated by the group and wanted to understand more about them.

He hesitated, wondering if he should make a move and approach the guys. His heart raced and his palms grew sweaty as he battled with his internal conflict. A part of him craved the sense of belonging that came with being a part of their group, but another part feared the potential consequences of diving into that world.

"Maybe if I just get closer, listen in on their conversations, I can learn more about them," Jason reasoned with himself. With that thought, he mustered up the courage to take a few steps closer, trying not to draw too much attention to himself.

As he inched nearer, the gang members briefly noticed Jason's presence. They exchanged glances, silently acknowledging the observer, before quickly returning their attention to their banter and laughter. Jason lingered nearby, attempting to catch snippets of their conversation and study their interactions. His desire to belong grew stronger with each passing moment, yet he still hesitated, unsure whether to approach the group or retreat back into the shadows.

Suddenly, Ryan's voice broke through Jason's thoughts. "Hey man, you gonna join us or just keep standing there?" he asked.

Jason took a deep breath before pushing himself to move closer towards the group of people. The sound of their loud conversations and laughter urged him to be part of them. He felt a hint of hope as stepped closer, ready to accept the challenge of mingling with the crowd.

The acrid smell of cigarette smoke mingled with the electric hum of the arcade machines as Jason approached the group, their laughter and banter a siren call that drew him in. Ryan, John, Eric, and Tom were gathered around the latest Mortal Kombat game, their fingers tapping furiously on the buttons, their eyes locked onto the screen.

"Man, that was easy money last night," John bragged, his country drawl unmistakable even over the din of the arcade. "That fool didn't even see it coming."

"Right?" agreed Ryan, his voice buzzing with energy. "We got away clean, too. No one will ever know it was us." His short, scrawny frame seemed to vibrate with excitement, fueled by adrenaline and whatever substances coursed through his veins.

Eric abruptly reminded everyone of the street fight with a gang from across town, his voice filled with a slight undertone of challenge. He wanted to demonstrate that he wasn't just John's follower; he could hold his own in any situation.

"Damn straight!" Tom exclaimed, his preppy veneer cracking for a moment as he landed a punch on the rival character in the game. "They won't be messing with us again anytime soon."

As Jason absorbed their words, he began to envision himself as part of their stories - standing shoulder to shoulder with these young renegades, united by loyalty and a shared defiance of authority. His pulse quickened at the thought, sending a thrill coursing through his veins that he couldn't quite shake off. It was a thrilling, dangerous fantasy - one that seemed to beckon to him with every passing moment.

Jason watched from the sidelines, taking in their camaraderie and loyalty, even as they discussed their criminal exploits. Despite their rough edges, there was something magnetic about this group, a sense of belonging that he craved. They were like a family, bound together by shared experiences and secrets, a world apart from Jason's own isolated upbringing.

"Man, I could do this all day!" Ryan declared, his voice crackling with energy as he slammed his palm down on the machine, claiming another victory. His scrawny frame belied an almost frenetic strength, fueled by some unknown force that kept him in constant motion. Even standing still, he seemed poised on the edge of action, ready to spring into a fight or defend his friends at a moment's notice.

"Ease up, man," John drawled, leaning against the wall with a lazy grin. Despite his laid-back demeanor, there was something dangerous lurking beneath the surface, a cunning mind always scheming for shortcuts and opportunities. He seemed to live for the thrill of bending the rules, the satisfaction of getting one over on the world that had tried to hold him down.

"Whatever, John," Ryan shot back playfully, rolling his eyes as he turned back to the game. "You're just jealous 'cause you can't keep up."

"Keep telling yourself that," John replied, a smirk tugging at the corners of his mouth as he nudged Eric, who stood nearby with Tom, watching the game unfold.

Jason watched from his hiding spot, captivated by the easy banter, the shared laughter, the inside jokes that flowed effortlessly between the gang members. It was a world he longed to be a part of, a place where he could finally belong. But how? How could he bridge the gap between his sheltered existence in the suburbs and their gritty reality?

As the gang continued to enjoy their afternoon at the arcade, Jason found himself analyzing each of their interactions, searching for clues that might help him make that leap. He watched as Ryan's boundless energy seemed to infect those around him, drawing them in like moths to a flame. He observed John's knack for making even the most mundane activities feel like an adventure, turning every obstacle into a challenge to be overcome.

Jason hovered nearby, trying to seem casual as he pretended to take interest in a pinball machine. His ears strained to catch bits of their conversation, his mind piecing together fragments of stories about late-night escapades and daring confrontations with rival gangs. As he listened, an intense longing swelled within him, fueled by a desire for camaraderie and excitement that seemed so foreign compared to his own mundane existence.

"Damn, bro, you're on fire today!" Eric called out to Ryan, clapping him on the back as he scored yet another win. His words were casual, but the pride in his voice was unmistakable – a loyalty that ran deep, binding them together like family.

"Ha! You know it," Ryan replied, grinning broadly. "Nobody can touch me when I'm in the zone."

"Except for me, of course," Tom added with a grin, pushing off from the wall and stepping up to the machine. "C'mon, let's see what you've really got."

"Bring it on!" Ryan challenged, his eyes gleaming with excitement as he prepared to face off against his friend.

"Man, y'all ain't got nothing on me!" Eric boasted, his lanky form hunched over the controls, eyes locked onto the screen.

"Shut up, Eric," Tom grumbled good-naturedly, rolling his eyes but allowing a grin to tug at the corners of his mouth. "You're not even that good."

"Whatever, man," Eric scoffed, undeterred by Tom's teasing. "You'll see when I beat your ass."

Jason remained rooted to the spot, his heart pounding in his chest as he drank in the scene before him. It was more than just a game; it was a glimpse into a world of unwavering loyalty and unbreakable bonds. And despite the warnings that echoed in the back of his mind, he couldn't deny the allure of that world, the irresistible pull of a place where he might finally find the belonging he so desperately craved.

Jason's gaze lingered on the gang, his curiosity piqued as he observed their camaraderie. He knew he should be wary, that getting involved with people like them could lead to trouble. Yet, the magnetic pull of their laughter and banter tugged at a part of him that longed for connection, for a place where he belonged.

"God, what am I even thinking?" Jason muttered under his breath, shaking his head as if to dispel the tempting thoughts. But still, he couldn't tear his eyes away from the group.

"Hey, you gonna stand there all day or you gonna play?" John called out suddenly, smirking as he caught sight of Jason watching them. The other gang members glanced over, sizing him up with interest.

"Uh..." Jason hesitated, his heart hammering in his chest as he considered his options. A moment of reckoning seemed to hang in the air – would he take the plunge and approach the gang, or retreat to the safety of his familiar world?

"Come on, cuz," Ryan encouraged, his voice laced with excitement. "Let's see what you've got."

"Alright, alright," Jason finally conceded, mustering the courage to step closer to the group. The decision felt dangerous, exhilarating – a taste of the life he'd been trying so hard to resist. It was a small choice, but one that carried the weight of potential consequences.

"Sure, why not?" Jason said, sounding more confident than he felt. He took a deep breath, pushing the doubts to the back of his mind as he approached the gang. What harm could it do, after all? It was just a game. As Jason stepped up to the controls, his heart pounding in his chest, he couldn't help but wonder what it would be like to be a part of their world. To know that someone had your back, no matter what. To be a part of something greater than himself.

With a deep breath, Jason grasped the joystick and began to play, his fingers moving almost instinctively over the buttons. As the game unfolded before him, he felt the weight of the gang's eyes on him, watching, evaluating. And for a moment, he allowed himself to believe that maybe, just maybe, he could find a place among them.

"Nice move!" Ryan shouted as Jason's character landed a finishing blow, earning a cheer from the others.

As the adrenaline coursed through his veins, Jason couldn't help but feel a sense of belonging, a connection to these outcasts who had carved out a place for themselves in the world. But deep down, a small voice whispered warnings of danger, urging him not to lose himself in the allure of the gang.

"Hey, man," Eric said, nudging John with a grin. "Looks like our boy here's got some skills."

"About time he showed up to play," John replied, his troublemaking tendencies evident in the smirk that played on his lips.

Jason's heart pounded in his chest, the adrenaline coursing through him as he kept up with the gang in their game. Around him, the once-loud arcade seemed to fade into the background, leaving only the banter of his newfound friends and the blips of the video game. His desire to belong had never felt this strong before, and as he exchanged jokes with them, he couldn't help but feel a sense of acceptance.

"Alright, guys," Tom announced after a particularly intense round. "I gotta split. Catch you all later."

"Later, man," the others chorused, their easy camaraderie making it clear that this was not an unusual occurrence. As Tom disappeared into the crowd, Jason found himself holding his breath, unsure of his place in their tight-knit group now that they were one member short.

"Yo, cuz," Ryan addressed him, his energetic personality seeming to fill the void Tom's departure had left. "You're with us now, right?"

"Uh... yeah," Jason stammered, taken aback by the directness of the question. He could feel the weight of their gazes once more, as if they were trying to assess his loyalty and commitment.

"Good," John chimed in, clapping him on the back. "We've got something important coming up, and we could use someone with your talents."

"Something important?" Jason echoed, his curiosity piqued. He knew that getting involved with the gang meant venturing into uncharted territory - but what exactly did they have planned? And did he truly want to be a part of it?

"Let's just say," Eric said with a cryptic smile, "that it's going to be a night to remember. Are you in or out?"

Jason hesitated for a moment, the weight of the decision heavy on his shoulders. His pulse quickened at the thought of crossing that line, of fully immersing himself in their world. The shadows seemed to call out to him, whispering warnings and urging him to retreat to the safety of his old life.

"Jason?" Ryan prompted, his voice laced with anticipation. "What's it gonna be, man?"

"Alright," Jason finally replied, swallowing hard as he made up his mind. "I'm in."

"Welcome to the crew," John said with a grin, sealing Jason's fate with those four simple words.

As they walked away from the arcade together, leaving behind the flashing lights and din of sounds, Jason couldn't help but wonder if he'd just taken a step towards something thrilling - or something that would change his life forever.

—-

2

The First Meet-Up

"Yo, Jason, come meet the crew," Tom called out to me as I looked back one last time at my old life, still visible through the chain-link fence that separated our turf from the rest of the world.

"Alright, let's do this," I said with a mix of excitement and apprehension. Tom led me down a narrow alley, filled with graffiti and the stench of stale urine. As we approached a small neighborhood park, I found myself in front of a small gathering of teenagers, chatting and laughing amongst themselves.

"Guys, this is Jason," Tom announced, and the group's attention shifted to me. I could feel their eyes appraising me, sizing me up.

"Jason, this here's Calisto" – he pointed at a stunning Pacific island girl who couldn't have been more than fifteen– "Consuelo" – a younger Mexican girl who seemed eager to fit in – "Cynthia" – Consueolo's older sister, about sixteen, with beautiful long black hair – "Rachel" – a tomboyish girl with an undeniable beauty – "Finally, that's Kathy." Tom indicated towards a petite white girl sitting near the window, her hair pulled back into braids. She looked up at Jason, offering a sheepish smile. "She's my little sister, so watch yourself around her."

"Hey," I mumbled sheepishly, unsure of how to act in front of these strangers who were supposed to become my new family.

"Sup, man," Calisto replied casually, giving me a nod. The others echoed similar greetings, but I could tell they were still guarded, still unsure of what to make of me.

"Alright, now that we're all acquainted, let's get this party started!" Tom declared, pulling out a bottle of cheap liquor from his backpack.

"Drink up, J" – Rachel handed me a red plastic cup filled with an amber liquid –"Don't worry, it ain't gonna kill you."

"Thanks," I said, taking a cautious sip. The liquid burned my throat, but I tried my best not to show it, not wanting to seem weak in front of my potential new friends. I had never had alcohol before, but I didn't want to appear inexperienced.

"Come on, let's see what you got," Calisto said, challenging me with a grin as she grabbed my hand and pulled me toward the makeshift dance floor that was nothing more than a patch of dirt surrounded by graffiti-covered walls.

"Uh, I'm not much of a dancer," I confessed, feeling the heat rise to my cheeks.

"Neither are any of these guys," she replied, laughing as she pointed at Tom and the others who were dancing to some 90's hip-hop music blaring from the old boombox. "Don't worry about it. Just have fun." The rhythms of the gangster rap pulsed through me like a second heartbeat, and the words that filled my head felt like an inner monologue. The music was like a source of energy, propelling me further than before.

"Alright," I conceded, letting Calisto lead me into the fray. As we danced, I couldn't help but feel a connection with Calisto. She moved gracefully, her whole body becoming one with the music. I felt like we were somehow kindred spirits brought together by fate. The evening faded quickly as we moved to the beat and my worries of fitting into this new group of strangers melted away until I felt like I had known them forever.

"Maybe this isn't so bad after all," I thought to myself as I looked around at my new crew, each one of them seemingly accepting me into their fold without hesitation. For the first time in a long time, I felt like I belonged somewhere, like I had a purpose. Little did I know how much my life would change from that moment on.

We moved on from the park, and headed to Cynthia and Consuelo's house just down the road. The sun dipped low in the sky, casting a warm orange glow across the dilapidated party house. The cracked walls were adorned with graffiti, and the broken windows gaped like missing teeth. A small wooden fence surrounded the rear of the property, as much to keep people out as to keep us in. This was our sanctuary, our escape from the world outside.

"Hey, you gotta meet my little brothers!" Cynthia shouted over the pulsing rhythm of music that filled the air. She led me to a corner where two young boys huddled together, playing with a battered deck of cards. Their clothes were worn and stained, but their faces were bright and animated.

"Jason, this is Jessie, he's six and Johnnie, he's eight," she said, her voice softening as she ruffled the hair of the six-year-old. "Boys, this is Jason. He's new around here."

"Hi, Jason!" Jessie exclaimed with a toothy grin, while Johnnie gave me a shy nod of acknowledgment.

"Hey, guys," I replied, trying to sound friendly and approachable. "Nice to meet you both."

I could see the weight of responsibility on Cynthia and Consuelo's shoulders as they looked after their younger siblings. It made me want to prove myself to them even more, to show that I could be a dependable part of their lives.

"Watch this," I said, pulling a quarter from my pocket. With a practiced flick of my wrist, I made it seem as though the coin had disappeared into thin air. Both boys' eyes widened in amazement as I revealed the coin once again, tucked behind Jessie's ear.

"Whoa! How'd you do that?" Johnnie asked, his shyness momentarily forgotten.

"Magic," I teased, winking at him. Inside, I felt a surge of pride at being able to impress and bond with the boys, bringing a moment of happiness to their tough lives.

"Hey, Jason," Calisto called from across the yard. "You play basketball?"

"Uh, yeah!" I replied, eager for another opportunity to show off my skills. "I play pick up games here and there."

"Perfect! We're short one player for our game. You can join us," she said, gesturing toward a makeshift court with a lopsided hoop.

The gang had set up a rough-and-tumble version of a basketball court in the backyard, using old milk crates and scrap wood for the backboards. As the game began, I focused on playing well, hoping to earn their respect through my athletic abilities.

"Nice shot, Jason!" Rachel cheered as I sunk a three-pointer from behind a cracked line on the concrete.

"Thanks!" I grinned, feeling a swell of pride at their approval.

In between games, we shared stories about our lives and experiences. I talked about growing up without many friends. I told them about the times I got into fights at school, defending myself against a bully. They listened intently, nodding in understanding and offering words of encouragement.

"Sounds like you've had it tough too," Kathy remarked, her voice thick with empathy. "But we've all got each other's backs here."

As the sun disappeared below the horizon and the warm glow of the party house dimmed, I felt a growing sense of belonging. These people, this place – they offered me something I hadn't found anywhere else: acceptance, friendship, and a purpose to protect those around me. And in that moment, I knew I would do whatever it took to prove myself worthy of their trust.

A few days after the basketball game, I found myself back at the party house, watching an intense game of dominoes between Calisto and Consuelo. The other gang members were scattered around the room, some playing cards, others deep in conversation. As I leaned against the wall, I noticed that their initial skepticism towards me had begun to fade, replaced by a cautious acceptance.

"Hey Jason, you wanna jump in on the next game?" Calisto asked, her dark eyes glinting as she placed a domino down with a satisfying click.

"Sure," I replied, feeling a surge of excitement at being included. I took a seat beside her, trying not to let my nervousness show.

"Alright, man, just watch and learn," she winked, playfully nudging my shoulder. "I'm about to school Consuelo over here."

As we played, I found myself growing more and more comfortable in their presence. Laughter filled the air, banter was exchanged, and even though I was still something of an outsider, they treated me as if I belonged. It wasn't long before I started to pick up on their slang and mannerisms, and I felt a newfound sense of pride in being part of this tight-knit group.

"Jason, you're getting better at this," Cynthia teased after I'd won a round. "Maybe you're not so bad after all."

"Thanks," I mumbled, warmth spreading through my chest at the compliment. Despite my past experiences of mistrust and isolation, I could feel the walls I'd built around myself beginning to crumble.

In the following days, Calisto and I spent more time together, our connection deepening with each shared moment. We'd stay up late into the night talking about our dreams and fears, often losing track of time as we confided in one another.

"Y'know, Jason," Calisto said one night as we lounged on the roof, gazing up at the stars, "I never thought I'd meet someone like you. You're different from most guys around here."

"Is that a good thing?" I asked, my heart pounding in my chest.

"Definitely," she replied, her voice soft and sincere. "You've got this vulnerability about you, but also a strength that's just waiting to be unleashed. I think that's why everyone's starting to trust you – they can see it too."

As I lay there beside her, the cool breeze rustling through my hair, I felt a weight lift from my shoulders. For the first time in my life, I was seen for who I truly was – not just a tall, lanky kid with a tough exterior, but someone with dreams and aspirations, with a desire to belong and protect those he cared about. And as I looked over at Calisto, her dark eyes reflecting the moonlight, I knew that I'd finally found that elusive sense of belonging I'd been searching for all along.

We joined the others back in the house. "Jason, my man!" Calisto grinned as she clapped a hand on my shoulder. "You're one of us now. Officially."

My heart swelled with excitement and relief at her words. I glanced around the dimly lit room, taking in the faces of my newfound family – Calisto, Consuelo, Cynthia, Rachel, and Kathy – each nodding their approval. I felt like I had been holding my breath for weeks, waiting for this moment, and now I could finally exhale.

Surrounded by these newfound allies, I could feel my confidence begin to swell. But while they all welcomed me with open arms, I noticed that the girls didn't always receive the same respect as the boys. They were oftentimes referred to as hoodrats and treated like possessions rather than people. I was determined to make sure this would not be their fate under my watch. I made it a priority to show the girls in our group that they were valued and protected. When we'd go out in public or to parties, I'd make sure none of the guys messed with them. If anyone gave them trouble, I was there to step in and make things right. Whenever they needed anything, I'd chip in what little money I had just so they wouldn't have to worry. It felt good knowing that at least in my small corner of the world, there were some people who respected and cared for one another. And it wasn't long before word got around about what kind of person I was – someone who valued loyalty above all else and would always have his friends' backs no matter what. It was a reputation I was proud to have gained and one that served me well over the months as our gang continued to grow and thrive despite its tumultuous beginnings. From then on, my loyalty and commitment never waivered – even when things got tough, even when others doubted me or tried to bring me down. No matter how difficult it became, I never lost sight of who I truly was or forgot why we were all fighting for something better: family, respect, strength, unity — words which now held new meaning for me as they echoed through my mind each night before sleep took over.

18

"Thanks, guys," I said, trying to sound casual, but unable to hide the emotion in my voice. "I won't let you down."

Calisto leaned in, her eyes locked on mine. "We know you won't," she said, giving me a knowing smile. "Now let's celebrate!"

As the gang erupted into cheers and laughter, I took a moment to drink in the scene unfolding before me. This motley crew, with their shared experiences and unbreakable bonds, had taken me in without hesitation, showing me a sense of loyalty and belonging that I'd never known before. And now, it was my turn to prove myself worthy of their trust.

"Hey, Jason," Rachel called out from across the room, a wicked grin on her face. "How 'bout you show us what you got?

As her words echoed, I had to ponder what she meant. Suddenly, Ryan appeared and pounded my face with a fist. Cheers came from the people around us as they shouted "Fight! Fight!" Not in my wildest dreams did I think I would be part of a gang initiation like this. Luckily, I was able to regain my composure quickly and fight back, throwing a few punches of my own. He attempted to throw a right hook but I seized the opportunity and tackled him to the ground, landing blow after blow and grappling with him for several minutes. Finally, it was all over.

Ryan rose and offered a hand to help me up. "Welcome, brother!" he said. Tom came closer and presented me with a blue cloth, which I was instructed to tuck into my back right pocket. "When you take this rag, it symbolizes your allegiance to us, and ours to you. You can never undo the connection; we will be family until the final day comes."

"Damn right!" Calisto chimed in, raising her 40 ounce in toast. "To our new brother and protector!"

The room filled with the clink of bottles and the warmth of solidarity as we toasted our newfound unity. But beneath the surface of the celebration, I couldn't help but think about the responsibility that now weighed on my shoulders. My need to protect my new family was fierce, an instinct born from a deep sense of loyalty and purpose.

"Hey, Calisto," I whispered, leaning in closer to her. "I'm serious about what I said earlier – if you ever need me, I'll be there."

"Same goes for you, Jason," she replied, her dark eyes meeting mine with unwavering sincerity. "You're one of us now, and we've got your back."

The words echoed in my mind, filling me with determination. No matter what challenges lay ahead, I'd face them head-on, with my newfound family by my side. I'd never felt more alive, more connected, or more ready to prove myself. This was just the beginning.

When the moon began to ascend and the mist of the evening came in, I stood beside my new family on the cracked pavement outside our party house. The scent of charred meat from a nearby barbecue filled the air, mingling with laughter and the pulsing beat of bass-heavy music. My heart pounded against my chest with excitement, each rhythmic thud a reminder that I was finally where I belonged.

"Jason! You're up!" Calisto called out to me from her spot by the makeshift grill, tossing me a pair of tongs. I caught them with ease, stepping forward to take my place behind the smoky haze. As I flipped burgers and hotdogs for my hungry comrades, I couldn't help but feel a newfound sense of purpose.

"Hey, these are pretty good," Rachel remarked between bites, nodding appreciatively in my direction. "You've got some skills, man."

"Thanks," I replied, flashing her a grin. "Anything for my family."

"Speaking of family," Consuelo interjected as she approached, her gaze drifting toward her little brothers Jessie and Johnnie playing tag nearby. "We've got to watch out for those two. They've been talking about wanting to join the gang when they grow up."

"Really?" I frowned, my eyes narrowing with concern. "They're just kids."

"Yeah, well, it's not like we have a lot of other options around here," Cynthia chimed in, her voice tinged with bitterness. "What else are they supposed to look up to?"

I swallowed hard, a knot forming in my stomach. Images of Jessie and Johnnie, wide-eyed and innocent, being drawn into this dangerous life weighed heavily on my conscience. In that moment, I knew that my role as protector needed to extend beyond my immediate circle – I had a responsibility to do what I could to shield these children from the harsh reality of our world. Even though I discovered what I was searching for, a nagging sense of guilt washed over me as I gazed at the innocent little boys. This lifestyle would not do them any favors in life. In the back of my head, I knew that peril and wickedness were coming their way, and I prayed that they'd find a way out or, better yet, find something else to live for besides this life.

"Maybe we can show them there's more to life than just the gang," I suggested, my voice soft but resolute. "Help them see that they have other choices."

"Like what?" Calisto questioned, her brow furrowed with doubt. "We're all trapped here, one way or another."

"Maybe," I conceded, my gaze fixed on the horizon as darkness slowly enveloped the sky. "But maybe we can find a way out – together."

The silence that followed was heavy, and I could feel the weight of their thoughts as they considered my words. We all knew the consequences of this life, the risks and sacrifices it demanded of us. But perhaps, in some small way, we could forge a new path for ourselves and those who came after us.

"Let's do it," Calisto finally said, determination flickering in her eyes like a spark ready to ignite. "Let's show them there's more to life than this. Let's fight for a better future – whatever it takes."

As we stood there, united by a common goal, I couldn't help but feel an overwhelming sense of belonging. This was my family now, and I'd do everything in my power to protect them – even if it meant facing the challenges and consequences that lay ahead, together.

Hours later, when the sun began to rise, we said our goodbyes as everyone went their separate ways. As I drove home, a smile was plastered on my face. I knew that things were finally starting to look up for me in this new life.

3

A First Love

The following night, Jason was excited to leave the arcade and rush over to Cynthia and Consuelo's place, his second home. As he exited his lowrider truck, the distant sound of laughter and music reached his ears, signaling another night of revelry awaited him. As he approached, Calisto leaned against the porch railing, her long dark hair cascading over her shoulders like a waterfall. Her eyes sparkled as they met his, a warmth emanating from her that drew him in.

"Hey, Jason," she greeted him, a hint of shyness creeping into her voice. "Glad you could make it tonight."

"Wouldn't miss it for the world," he replied, grinning as he ascended the steps to join her on the porch.

Inside, the party was in full swing, with gang members mingling, drinking, and dancing. Jason navigated the crowded room, stopping to exchange pleasantries with various members. As he made his way back to Calisto, he could feel the subtle shift in the atmosphere. It was no secret that she had once been John's girlfriend, and Jason's growing affection for her was stirring undercurrents of tension within the gang.

"Yo, J!" called out Cynthia, her voice cutting through the chatter. She waved him over, her dark eyes sparkling with excitement. "Come meet the big guns!"

Jason approached the group, feeling a mixture of apprehension and curiosity. At the center of the circle stood two men, both exuding an air of power and danger. The first was Spoon, a 21-year-old black guy built like a boxer. His muscles rippled beneath his tight-fitted shirt, and an intimidating scowl perpetually etched on his face. Rumor had it that he once took down five guys in a street brawl singlehandedly – his reputation as someone not to be messed with was well-earned.

"Sup," Spoon grunted, sizing Jason up. He didn't bother extending a hand in greeting, but there was something about his intense gaze that told Jason he had the gang leader's attention.

"Hey," Jason replied cautiously, trying to project confidence despite the butterflies in his stomach. He knew that to be accepted by this group, he couldn't show any sign of weakness.

Beside Spoon stood Nate, an 18-year-old white guy with a small stature that belied his penchant for violence. While not as physically imposing as his counterpart, there was a cold, calculating glint in his eyes that sent shivers down Jason's spine. Nate was known for being unpredictable, and his volatile temper had earned him a fearsome reputation within the gang.

"New blood, huh?" Nate smirked, looking Jason up and down with a predatory gleam in his eyes. "What makes you think you can hang with us?"

Jason swallowed hard, forcing himself to maintain eye contact with the intimidating figure before him. "I'm tired of being alone," he admitted, his voice steady despite the pounding in his chest. "I want to be a part of something bigger than myself."

"Is that right?" Spoon asked skeptically, crossing his arms over his broad chest. "You willing to put in the work, prove yourself to us? Loyalty's everything here."

Jason nodded, determination shining in his eyes. "Whatever it takes," he replied, his voice firm.

"Good," Nate said, a wicked grin spreading across his face. "We will see what you're made of."

Night after night, Jason found himself at Cynthia and Consuelo's house, the gang's usual gathering spot. The air was always thick with the scent of stale beer, hard alcohol, and a mixture of drugs that clouded the room. Jason had never been one to partake in the substances, but he couldn't deny the sense of togetherness that surrounded him as the gang laughed and bonded over shared experiences.

"Yo, J, grab yourself a drink!" Spoon called out to him from across the room, a smirk playing on his lips as he noticed Jason standing awkwardly in the doorway. "You ain't gonna last long around here if you don't loosen up a little."

"Thanks, man," Jason replied, forcing a smile as he made his way over to the makeshift bar set up in the corner of the living room. He grabbed a half-empty bottle of cheap vodka, pouring a shot for himself before rejoining the others. He winced as the liquid burnt its way down his throat, but he felt a small sense of pride at having successfully integrated himself into this new world.

The parties at Cynthia and Consuelo's house were a far cry from anything Jason had experienced in his previous life. They were wild, reckless affairs, fueled by a potent mix of alcohol, drugs, and adrenaline. But amidst the chaos, there was an undeniable sense of unity that drew Jason in, making him feel like he truly belonged for the first time in his life.

Cynthia's mom, Jackie, was a local escort who turned a blind eye to her daughters' involvement with the gang. It wasn't uncommon to see her flitting about the house, scantily clad and all too happy to join in on the festivities. Though she rarely interacted with her children directly, it was clear that she didn't have any qualms about their chosen lifestyle. Cynthia was the eldest of the children, and she had been thrust into the role of surrogate parent when her mother's job as an escort kept her away for hours, and sometimes days at a time. She was only sixteen but took it upon herself to care for her three younger siblings, often going without food so that they could have enough to eat. Money was tight in their household, and Cynthia constantly fretted about how they would make ends meet. Still, she made sure there was always a home-cooked meal on the table and looked after her siblings with an unwavering sense of responsibility. Even though she was young, she had already taken on more responsibilities than most adults ever have. As Cynthia settled into her role as head of the household, Jason started to become a regular presence. He quickly proved himself to be a hard worker with a strong moral code – qualities that were respected by everyone in the gang. He began helping out around the house; doing whatever he could to ease the burden on Cynthia and her family. Soon enough, Jason found himself held in high esteem by both Cynthia and Consuelo for his dependability and loyalty. Together they partied late into the night, enjoying each other's company and creating lasting memories that no one else understood or could replicate. Jason felt at home within this new family; something he never expected or thought possible before coming here. He knew he would do anything for them – even if it meant putting his own life in danger – because this gang was no longer just an organization but also his chosen family.

"Hey, Jason," Consuelo said, sidling up next to him as he stared at the chaotic scene unfolding before him. "You're not like the others, you know?"

"Is that a bad thing?" Jason asked, his brow furrowing slightly as he met her gaze.

"No," she replied, shaking her head emphatically. "It's just... different. You don't do the drugs, and you seem to really care about everyone here."

"Someone has to, right?" Jason responded with a shrug, a small smile playing on his lips. "We're all in this together."

"Thanks for looking out for us," Consuelo whispered, giving his hand a quick squeeze before disappearing back into the crowd.

"Jason, man, can I talk to you outside?" John asked, his usually friendly demeanor replaced by a cold seriousness.

Jason let out a single word in response, "Sure," and followed John down the creaky stairs of the porch. With each step he took, his stomach turned into more and more of a tangled mess as he wondered whether a physical altercation was about to start.

John cleared his throat and shifted uncomfortably, hands moving to rub the back of his neck. "I'm aware that you and Calisto have grown close," he said. "And I just want you to know that I don't have any hard feelings about it. But some of the guys... well, they're not too happy."

Jason's heart pounded in his chest as he considered John's words. He knew the stakes were high, and the last thing he wanted was to create discord within the gang he'd come to see as his family.

"John, I respect you," he said earnestly. "And I don't want to cause any problems. But I care about Calisto, and I think she feels the same way."

"Listen, I'm not trying to stand in your way," John replied, his tone softening. "But if you're going to be with her, you need to be ready to protect her. And all of us too. We need to know we can trust you."

Jason met John's gaze, his determination evident in the depths of his blue eyes. "You can trust me," he assured him. "I'll do whatever it takes to keep our group safe. You have my word."

Over the next few days, Jason worked tirelessly to prove his loyalty to the gang. He mediated disputes, offered support and advice, and put himself in harm's way when necessary, all to protect those he now considered family. His unwavering dedication eventually won over even the most skeptical members, and the turmoil surrounding his relationship with Calisto began to fade.

As they sat together on the porch one evening, Calisto curled against Jason's side, her head resting on his shoulder. "You've really become our protector," she murmured, her voice filled with admiration. "Thank you for being there for us."

"Calisto, I'd do anything for you and the gang," Jason whispered, his arm wrapped protectively around her. "This is where I belong, and I will always be here to keep you all safe."

With that promise, Jason solidified his place within the gang, earning their trust and forging an unbreakable bond. Little did he know the challenges that lay ahead, and the lengths he would go to uphold his commitment to them.

Jason leaned against the graffiti-covered walls of Cynthia and Consuelo's house, taking in the sight of his newfound family. Spoon, the intimidating gang leader, laughed as he playfully punched one of the younger members, breaking the tension that had lingered from days prior.

"Hey, man," Nate, the other leader, called out to Jason with a grin. "You think you can handle another round of sparring? I'm itching to see what you got."

Jason shrugged, a cocky smile playing at the corners of his mouth. "Why not?

But don't blame me when you get your ass kicked."

Nate let out a laugh and shook his head. "We'll see about that cuz."

As they squared off, the gang gathered around, cheering and placing bets on the outcome. The air buzzed with comradeship, and Jason felt a sense of belonging that had been absent for so long. When the match began, Nate threw the first punch, but Jason easily dodged it and countered with a swift jab of his own, knocking Nate down. Before Nate had a chance to recover, Jason had him pinned to the ground. The gang erupted into cheers, impressed by Jason's quick reflexes and skill.

Spoon clapped Jason on the back in congratulations while the others gathered around to congratulate him as well. "You got some real talent there," Spoon said with a nod. "Not many people can take down Nate that fast."

Jason smiled modestly as he stood up and offered his hand to help Nate back up off the ground. "Thanks," he said simply, though his eyes sparkled with pride.

That night, as everyone prepared to head out, Cynthia and Consuelo insisted that Jason stay over at their place instead of returning to his own home. After what he'd done for them all day, they felt like it was the least they could do in return.

Jason gratefully accepted their invitation and settled in next to Calisto on an old mattress Cynthia had set up for him in one corner of the room. As they drifted off to sleep in each other's arms, Jason felt relieved and content for perhaps the first time since joining the gang. He'd finally found a family who would accept him no matter what—and better yet—a family who believed in him unconditionally.

As his connections with the gang deepened, so too did his relationship with Calisto. They spent countless hours together, talking about their lives before the gang, their dreams for the future, and the challenges they faced day to day. Calisto's unwavering support became a pillar of strength for Jason, as he navigated this new world.

"Calisto," Jason said one evening, as they sat on the porch under the moonlight. "I don't know what I would do without you. You've been there for me through everything, and I want to be that person for you too."

She smiled and squeezed his hand. "You already are, Jason. And I'm not going anywhere."

"Neither am I," he whispered, pulling her close.

Amidst the chaos and danger of their lifestyle, Jason found solace in the connections he'd made with the gang - and, most importantly, with Calisto. As they faced the uncertainties of life together, they knew they could rely on each other, no matter the obstacles that lay ahead.

Friday night soon approached, and like every Friday night, the streets of downtown were packed with teenagers driving their cars during cruising. Jason was the only one in his group that had a vehicle, so he offered to take everyone down to join the fun. The cab and bed of his lowrider truck filled up quickly with people as they took off for downtown. Jason's truck was the epitome of cool, a beloved icon among local teenagers. The beautiful teal Nissan truck had been lowered to the ground and adorned with chrome rims and neon lighting. It boasted a heart-pounding stereo system that commanded attention from blocks away. Jason also installed a television with a Nintendo 64, perfect for gaming on long drives. He always made sure the bed was stocked with cold drinks. All the members of the group had nicknames, and as Jason was the one with the wheels, they started calling him "Jayride".

Once they reached downtown, some other kids jumped in the truck as well. They drove up and down the streets, playing loud music while admiring each other's cars or flirting with passersby. Jason was in his element, effortlessly navigating the streets with skill. He felt a surge of pride as his friends shouted his nickname—"Jayride!"—every time he did a burn out, or raced a fellow car enthusiast. The night continued on like this for hours, until they decided to take a break and pull into an famous burger joint. The group spent the dinner talking and laughing over sodas and burgers before deciding to hit the road again. Carousing with buddies and enemies alike usually made it a lively time, however, sometimes rival gangs would appear and tempers flared leading to a brawl. This night happened to be one of those nights.

As they drove around, a member of a rival gang shouted derogatory comments at Jason, Spoon, who was sitting in the back of Jason's truck climbed out of the pickup and ran up to the banger's car. With one swift punch, he knocked him unconscious before quickly returning to the truck. Jason felt his heart racing but made sure not to show his fear. He glanced at Calisto, who had a look of concern on her face, and gave her a reassuring nod. She briefly squeezed his hand before letting go. Jason drove away in a hurry, gunshots ringing out behind him. He suspected it was the rival gang members trying to catch up with him and take him down. After executing some daring driving techniques, he managed to lose them. A police officer nearby heard the gun shots and noticed Jason's vehicle quickly exiting the area. The cop decided to pull Jason over for an investigation. Thankfully no one was hurt and after a lengthy questioning, they were released and went back to the party house.

After escaping the rival gang, Jason and his friends finally arrived back to the safety of Cynthia's house. As they got out of the truck, Calisto ran up to Jason and wrapped her arms around him, tears streaming down her face. She was relieved they had made it back safely. Everyone else in the group also expressed their appreciation for him leading them out of a potentially deadly situation.

Jason smiled down at Calisto and pulled her closer into a warm embrace. He was thankful for having such amazing people in his life that were willing to stand by his side no matter what. After the group had calmed down from the excitement and fear of their narrow escape, they all went inside Cynthia's house to celebrate with music and food.

In the dimly lit safe house, Jason sat on a worn-out sofa next to Calisto, their fingers intertwined as they listened to Spoon and Nate recount the latest exploits. The room buzzed with laughter and affinity, each member of the gang sharing stories, jokes, and even heartfelt confessions.

"Man, did you see that bitch drop with one hit?" Spoon chuckled, slapping his knee.

"Yeah, he's like a one hit wonder! " Nate laughed, wiping a tear away from his eye. "I thought you were gonna kill him!"

Jason laughed along with them, feeling a warmth and connection he'd never experienced before. He looked around at the ragtag group of misfits who had become his family, and a wave of gratitude washed over him. It wasn't so long ago that he'd been alone and adrift, unsure of his place in the world. But now, with these people by his side, he finally felt like he belonged.

"Hey, J," Calisto whispered, leaning in closer. "You know you saved us, right? We couldn't have made it through tonight without you."

"Yeah," Jason murmured, nodding as he met her gaze. "I know. And I'm here for all of you, no matter what."

"Good," she replied, giving his hand a reassuring squeeze. "Because we need you, Jason. You're our rock."

For the first time in his life, Jason understood what it meant to be needed, to be irreplaceable. With every daring mission and heart-pounding escape, he proved himself not only to the gang but also to himself. He was no longer the lonely teenager desperate for connection; he was a vital part of something bigger than himself. In the gang's eyes, he was a hero – and he was starting to believe it, too.

"Alright, guys," Spoon announced, clapping his hands together. "We had a close encounter tonight. Most likely, this is going to bring some heat on us. Jay, are you down?"

"Of course," he replied without hesitation, the thrill of anticipation coursing through him. "I'm ready for whatever comes our way."

"Damn right, you are," Nate chimed in, slapping Jason on the back. "Together, there's nothing we can't handle."

As they began to discuss what may be coming their way, Jason felt the excitement building within him. He knew that this life was dangerous, but with the gang by his side, he felt invincible. No challenge was insurmountable, no obstacle too great. This was where he was meant to be – and he couldn't wait to see what the future had in store for them all.

4

A New Family Forms

T he week stretched on like an eternity for Jason, while his friends lazed away their days, waiting for the weekend. He worked hard, he had an apartment to pay for, bills to cover, and he also had the added responsibility of taking care of the girls and the smaller boys. He worked like it was his last chance to ever show the world what he was capable of. Finally, the long awaited weekend arrived. His friends celebrated like it had been years since they last saw it, and Jason joined them, feeling his own relief. He allowed himself to rest, to sit back and relax for the first time in what felt like weeks. His body welcomed the embrace of the chair as he leaned back and watched the others laugh and dance with joy.

For a moment, Jason forgot all about his worries and the weight of the world that he carried on his shoulders. His friends surrounded him and nothing else seemed to matter. He took a deep breath and smiled, finally feeling content. The pounding bass from the stereo reverberated through the walls of the small, dimly lit home. Laughter and the mingling of voices filled the air, creating a chaotic symphony that was all too familiar. The smell of stale beer and smoke clung to everything, an ever-present reminder of the ongoing partying.

"Hey Jason!" yelled Ryan, his normally scrawny frame seeming to vibrate with energy, as he waved a half-empty bottle of Southern Comfort in the air. "You gotta try this stuff!"

He grabbed the bottle from Ryan, taking a swig before passing it on to John, who grinned as he drank.

"Man, we never stop partying, do we?" Eric said, his voice barely audible over the cacophony surrounding them. He leaned against the wall, trying hard to look relaxed despite the tension in his shoulders.

"Wouldn't be any fun if we did," Calisto replied, her eyes sparkling as she danced between Rachel and Cynthia. She threw her arms around Jason's neck, pulling him closer. "Besides, what's life without a little excitement?"

"Exactly," chimed in Consuelo, following her Cynthia's lead and joining the dance. Her movements were clumsy but enthusiastic, eager to prove herself to the older members of the gang.

"YO! Spoon just walked in!" Nate shouted from across the room, his face lighting up with excitement. Tom and Kathy exchanged a glance before heading over to greet him.

"Damn," Jason thought, "Spoon's presence changes everything." The atmosphere in the room seemed to shift, as if everyone felt the weight of their leader's arrival. "He's always been so violent; is this really the life I want?"

"Hey, man," Spoon called out, clapping Jason on the back with a force that almost knocked him over. "You've been doing good work lately. "

"Thanks, Spoon," Jason responded, trying to sound appreciative. But as he looked around at his so-called family, he couldn't help but feel a growing sense of unease.

"Hey, Jay," Rachel said, sidling up next to him and slipping her arm through his. "You okay? You seem kind of...distant tonight."

"Uh, yeah. Just thinking about some stuff," Jason admitted, forcing a smile.

"Thinking's for suckers!" exclaimed Ryan, punctuating his statement with a wild guffaw. "Just have another drink and live in the moment!"

"Maybe," Jason murmured, his thoughts turning inward once more. As the music pounded in his ears, and the laughter echoed around him, he began to question whether this life was truly worth the price it demanded.

The following day, Jason returned to his abode in a quaint five story brick building located in the low rent district of the city. He strolled down the hallway towards his residence and pushed open the door.

"Jason!" a voice called out from behind him. He turned to see Rachel and Calisto standing there, their eyes wide with fear and desperation. "They threw us out," Rachel explained, her voice cracking. "Our moms...they found out about everything." Consuelo peeked out from around the corner, she had decided to runaway with them.

"Damn," Jason muttered, taking in the sight of the three girls, looking small and vulnerable against the unforgiving darkness of the night. "Come on, you can crash at my place for now."

"Really?" Calisto asked, her voice barely above a whisper.

"Of course," Jason replied, offering a reassuring smile. "We're family, right?"

The four of them walked in silence towards Jason's apartment, the reality of what had just happened weighing heavily on all of them. Homeless and adrift, Rachel, Calisto, and Consuelo now looked to Jason as their protector. While he was no stranger to responsibility within the gang, this felt different – these were people he cared about, not just fellow members. As they arrived at his apartment, Rachel broke down into tears. "I don't know what we're gonna do," she said through sobs. "It's okay," Jason said softly, putting a comforting arm around her shoulder. "We'll figure something out." He ushered them inside and began to make arrangements for everyone to stay there until they could find somewhere else to go.

Jason knew he'd have to get a better job so he could support the girls while they got back on their feet again. Although it would be a long and difficult road ahead of them all, Jason couldn't help but feel a sense of pride in himself that he was able to provide for those who needed it most when nobody else could or would. Taking care of these girls was more than just part of gang life – it was part of being family.

Once inside, the small apartment seemed even more cramped than usual. Clothes and empty pizza boxes and Mountain Dew cans littered the floor, evidence of Jason's usually chaotic life. But in that moment, it became a sanctuary for the four of them.

"Thank you, Jason," Calisto said softly, her dark eyes shimmering with unshed tears. "I don't know what we would have done without you."

"Hey, it's no problem," Jason replied, trying to sound nonchalant despite the tightening in his chest. "Just doing what anyone in my position would do."

But as he watched Calisto settle into the makeshift bed he had created for her on the floor, he couldn't help but feel a growing attachment to her. Her vulnerability tugged at something deep within him, and he found himself wanting to protect her not just from the dangers of the streets, but also from the life they had all chosen.

"Calisto," he whispered, kneeling down next to her. "I know things are tough right now, but I promise you, I'll do everything I can to make sure you're safe."

"Jason, I…" she hesitated, searching for the right words. "I've been thinking about what's happened to us, and I don't know if this is the life I want anymore", referring to the violent and thuggish lifestyle they had grown accustomed to.

"Neither do I," Jason admitted, feeling a sense of relief wash over him as he realized he wasn't alone in his doubts. "But we're in this together now, and we'll figure it out – one step at a time."

He reached out and took her hand, their fingers intertwining like the threads of an uncertain future. As they lay there in the darkness, listening to the sounds of the city outside, it felt as though they were both standing on the edge of a precipice, unsure of what awaited them on the other side.

"Whatever happens, Calisto," Jason murmured, feeling a fierce determination rise within him. "I'll be here for you. Always."

"Thank you, Jason," she replied, her voice thick with emotion. "I know we'll find a way out of this…together." As their lips met, the couple's love blossomed and their relationship moved to the next level.

The following morning, sunlight streamed through the grimy windows, casting a warm glow across Jason's small apartment. He sat at the kitchen table with Rachel, Consuelo, and Calisto, their faces serious and solemn as he laid out his plan.

"Look, I know we've all been caught up in this gang life for too long," he began, his blue eyes determined. "But it doesn't have to be this way. We can change our lives, get out of this mess. We just need to make some smart choices."

Rachel shifted uncomfortably in her seat, her tomboyish features drawn tight with worry. Consuelo glanced nervously at her friends, seeking reassurance. But Calisto simply stared at Jason, her dark islander eyes filled with trust and love.

"First things first," Jason continued, "we need to get you guys back in school. Education is our ticket out of here, the key to building a better life for ourselves." The girls had not been in school all year and had missed much of what their fellow classmates were learning.

"Are you sure?" Consuelo asked hesitantly, her small Mexican frame leaning forward. "I mean, what if the other kids find out about our past?"

"Then we'll face it together," Jason replied firmly. "We can't let fear hold us back any longer."

The girls exchanged uncertain glances, but eventually nodded in agreement. They knew Jason was right – it was time to take control of their lives and leave the dangerous world of the gang behind.

A few days later, Jason drove Rachel, Consuelo, and Calisto to a school set up for runaway and homeless children, the tension palpable in the air. His grip on the steering wheel tightened as they passed the familiar haunts of their former lives – the liquor stores, the drug dens, the graffiti-covered walls that bore witness to countless acts of violence.

"Remember," he said, his voice steady, "we're doing this for our future. I have faith in you, I know you will all succeed! " The girls opened the door to a warm welcome from the team inside. All their needs were met; classes resumed, and they were fed and supported by their instructors and chaperones. As he drove back to his apartment, Jason felt a sense of satisfaction, knowing that the girls were safe at their new school. Although uncertain of how everything would turn out, he was still glad that he had been able to help them start fresh.

Later that day, Jason fetched the girls from school and started to drive them back to the apartment. As the truck pulled up to a traffic signal, it paused at a red light.

"Jason, look!" Calisto suddenly exclaimed, pointing to a van that had pulled up alongside them. A group of guys leaned out the windows, grinning and waving.

"Hey! You guys should come to a party we're having at the hotel tonight!" one of them shouted, his invitation laced with temptation.

"Uh, thanks, but we can't," Jason replied, trying to keep his voice casual as he focused on the road ahead. "We've got other plans."

"Suit yourselves but if you change your mind, it's at the hourly hotel on Division, room 211!" the guy called back, his laughter mocking as the car sped away.

Jason glanced furtively at the girls, knowing full well what they must be thinking. This was exactly the kind of scene they were trying to escape – the wild parties, the drugs, the alcohol. And yet, he could see the doubts creeping into their eyes, the allure of their old lives threatening to ensnare them once more.

"Listen," he said quietly, his heart pounding in his chest. "I know it's hard. But we have to stay strong. We have to fight for something better than this."

Against his better judgment, Jason found himself guiding the car towards the hotel where the party was being held. The girls' pleading and insistence had worn down his resolve, and he couldn't help but remember the intoxicating allure of those wild nights. 'Just one last time,' he thought. 'Then we'll leave it all behind.'

As they approached the hotel, an uneasy feeling settled in the pit of Jason's stomach. It spread like a slow poison, making him question the decision to come here. He glanced at Rachel, Consuelo, and Calisto, their faces alight with anticipation.

"Here goes nothing," he muttered as they stepped out of the truck and made their way to the room number told to them. As the door swung open, the blaring music and boisterous laughter hit them like a tidal wave. The room was packed with people, the air thick with the scent of alcohol and marijuana.

"Hey, look who decided to show up!" one of the partygoers called out, grinning at Jason and the girls. They smiled back hesitantly, trying to blend into the crowd. But as they moved further into the room, Jason noticed that something was off. Amidst the revelry, familiar faces from the rival gang stared back at him, and memories of the brutal fight from the cruising came flooding back. As Jason's eyes scanned the room, he saw an assault rifle and a black pistol laid out on the bed.

"Guys, I think we need to get out of here," he whispered urgently, grabbing the girls by their arms. But before they could make their move, one of the rival gang members shouted, "Yo, ain't that the crew from the other night?!"

The room fell silent, and all eyes turned to Jason and the girls. Adrenaline pumped through Jason's veins, his heart pounding in his chest. The rival gang members exchanged glances, and with a terrifying swiftness, they had their guns drawn and aimed at them.

"RUN!" Jason screamed, shoving Rachel, Consuelo, and Calisto towards the door. They sprinted down the hotel's exterior stairway, the sound of footsteps echoing behind them. Panic-stricken guests scrambled out of their way as they barreled past.

"Jason! The truck!" Calisto shrieked, her voice trembling with fear. Jason fumbled with the keys, his hands shaking uncontrollably. They quickly got into the truck, shutting the doors just in time to see two of their enemies running up. The rivals pounded on the drivers window with their fists as they drove away.

"Go, go, go!" Rachel yelled, her eyes wide with terror. Jason floored the accelerator, tires screeching against the pavement as they sped away from the hotel. His heart hammered against his ribcage, and his breathing was ragged.

"Is everyone okay?" he asked, his voice barely audible over the roar of the engine. The girls nodded, their faces pale and streaked with tears. As they put distance between themselves and the hotel, Jason couldn't help but feel the weight of responsibility on his shoulders. He had led them back into danger, and it was only by sheer luck that they had escaped unscathed. This time.

As they continued speeding away, Jason's mind raced at the same frantic pace as the truck. He couldn't shake the image of Rachel's tear-streaked face, or the way Consuelo had clung to Calisto in terror. And it was all because of him, because he'd allowed himself to be sucked into this life.

"Jason," Consuelo whispered, her voice shaking. "What are we going to do?"

"Keep driving," he responded, gripping the steering wheel so tightly his knuckles turned white. But as he said it, he realized he had no idea where they were going - not just in the truck, but in life itself.

"Is this what it's always going to be like?" Rachel asked, her voice barely audible. "Running from danger, never feeling safe?"

The question hung in the air, and Jason couldn't find an answer. He swallowed hard, a bitter taste filling his mouth. This wasn't the life he had imagined for himself, or for any of them. But how had he let it come to this?

"Being part of the gang... it was supposed to give us protection," Calisto said softly. "But now it feels like we need protection from the gang itself."

As the words settled over them like a dark cloud, Jason glanced at each of their faces in turn, seeing the fear that mirrored his own. The anger and loyalty that had once driven him to join the gang now seemed foolish, misguided. He had wanted a family, a sense of belonging, but at what cost?

"Maybe it's time to think about getting out," he said slowly, testing the words on his tongue. "We don't have to live like this."

"Can we really leave?" Consuelo asked, her eyes searching his for reassurance. "I mean, is there even a way out?"

"We'll make one," Jason replied, his voice firm. "I won't let anyone hurt you guys. I promise."

He knew that leaving the gang wouldn't be easy - they had a long and dangerous road ahead of them. But as he looked at Rachel, Consuelo, and Calisto, he realized that protecting them was more important than any misguided loyalty to a group that brought nothing but pain and chaos.

"Let's head back to my place," he suggested. "We'll figure things out from there."

"Jason," Calisto said quietly, reaching over to squeeze his hand. "Thank you."

"Of course," he whispered, allowing a small smile to break through the fear and uncertainty. It wasn't much, but it was a start. And for the first time in a long time, Jason felt a glimmer of hope that maybe, just maybe, they could find their way out of this darkness and into a better life.

The night was thick with tension as Jason and the girls returned to his apartment, the echo of fearful screams still ringing in their ears. The violent confrontation at the hotel had shaken them all to their core, a stark reminder of the potential consequences of their actions and the impact they had on not only their lives but those around them.

"Damn, that was too close," Calisto muttered as she sank onto Jason's worn couch, her fingers trembling. "We could've been killed."

"Those bastards were ready to shoot us down, they set us up." Rachel added, her voice laced with anger. "Just because we're part of this stupid gang."

"Hey, watch it," Jason warned, although his heart wasn't in it. He knew they were right. The gang life he'd become so entrenched in was tearing them apart. As he looked at the frightened faces of his makeshift family, he realized just how far they'd strayed from the life they'd once known.

"Jason, what are we going to do?" Consuelo asked, her dark eyes pleading. "We can't keep living like this."

He hesitated, his thoughts racing as he tried to formulate a plan. "I'm… I'm gonna talk to the guys," he said finally, determination setting in. "There has to be a way out. We have to make a change before it's too late."

"Are you sure, Jase?" Calisto asked, her voice wavering. "You know how they are. They might not let us go."

"Or worse, they'll come after us, you remember the oath, in it for life." Rachel added, shuddering.

"Then we'll deal with it," he replied, his voice firm. "But I can't stand by and watch our lives get destroyed anymore. This isn't us. It never was."

As Jason approached the gang's usual hangout spot, his heart hammered in his chest. He knew that the conversation he was about to have would likely put his life, and the lives of the girls, at risk. But he couldn't stand idly by any longer.

"Yo, Jase!" Spoon called out as Jason entered. "What's up, man?"

"Spoon, we need to talk," Jason said, trying to keep his voice steady. "In private."

"Sure thing, bro." Spoon led him to a corner, away from the others. "What's on your mind?"

"Look, man... Things have been getting really bad lately," Jason began, struggling to find the words. "I've been thinking a lot about what this life is doing to us – to Rachel, Consuelo, and Calisto. I don't want this for them or myself anymore."

"Jase, it's not like we're forcing you to be part of this," Spoon replied defensively. "But remember, you chose this life. You wanted in."

"I know," Jason admitted, his voice thick with emotion. "But I didn't realize what it would cost us. The violence, the fear... It's destroying us. We need to get out, Spoon. Please, just let us walk away."

"Walk away?" Spoon scoffed. "You think it's that easy? You think you can just turn your back on your family?"

"Is this really family, though?" Jason countered, desperation creeping into his voice. "Or is it just a bunch of people who care more about power and control than they do about each other?"

"Jase, you're talking crazy," Spoon snapped, his eyes narrowing. "You better watch yourself, or you'll end up regretting it."

"Maybe I already do," Jason whispered, his heart heavy with the weight of his decision. As he met Spoon's cold gaze, he knew that there was no turning back. He had to make a stand, for himself and those he cared about. And he could only hope that they would survive the fallout.

The tension in the room was palpable as Jason stared down at his trembling hands, the events of the hotel confrontation still fresh in his mind. The gang members had gathered around him, their eyes filled with a mixture of concern and suspicion.

"Jason, we get it," said Ryan, who had always been like a brother to him. "That shit was scary. But you can't let fear rule your life."

"Besides," added John, lounging on a nearby couch, "it's not like we go looking for trouble, man. We're just trying to survive out here. And together, we're stronger."

"Exactly," chimed in Cynthia, her arms crossed defiantly. "We've got each other's backs, no matter what. That's what family does."

Jason rubbed his temples, feeling the weight of their words. He knew they were right – the gang had been his support system since he could remember. Still, the images of Rachel, Consuelo, and Calisto cowering in terror from the rival gang members haunted him.

"Look, I know we're family," Jason began, his voice cracking slightly. "But I can't help but think about what our actions are doing to us – to Rachel, Consuelo, and Calisto. I don't want this for them or myself anymore."

"Look, man," Ryan said gently, placing a hand on Jason's shoulder. "You better think twice man. You know there's only one way out…" his words left to linger in the air.

Jason swallowed hard, nodding slowly as he stood up, feeling the weight of their collective gaze on him. He slipped out of the room, his heart pounding in his chest as he faced the most difficult decision of his life.

Would he choose loyalty to the gang that had been his family for so long? Or would he walk away, risking everything – including his own life – to protect those he cared for?

As Jason stepped into the night, the darkness seemed to swallow him whole, leaving him more uncertain than ever about the path that lay ahead.

The night air was cold, the moon casting a pale glow over the deserted streets as Jason walked aimlessly, lost in thought. The distant echo of sirens and barking dogs served as a constant reminder of the dangerous world he had become a part of. Every step carried the weight of his impending decision, the choice that would forever alter the course of his life.

"Hey, Jase," a familiar voice called out from behind. He turned to see Eric jogging towards him, his breath visible in the crisp air.

"Man, you left the meeting pretty quick," Eric said, concern evident in his voice. "Everything alright?"

Jason looked away, struggling to find the words. "I don't know, man," he finally admitted, his voice barely above a whisper. "I just... I can't keep going like this, you know? All the violence, the drinking... it's taking its toll."

Eric frowned, kicking at a stray pebble on the ground. "Look, I get it. But we're a family, right? We stick together, no matter what."

"But at what cost?" Jason asked, desperation creeping into his voice. "We almost got killed tonight, Eric. And for what? So we can prove we're tougher than some other gang?"

"Jase, you gotta understand. This is the life we chose. It ain't pretty, but it's ours," Eric insisted, gripping Jason's shoulder. "You walk away now, you're turning your back on all of us."

The conflict within Jason intensified, torn between loyalty to his gang family and the desire to protect those he cared about. Yet, he couldn't shake the growing sense of unease that plagued him since the hotel incident.

"Maybe there's another way," he suggested, more to himself than to Eric. "A way to take care of our own without all this violence."

"Man, if there was another way, don't you think we'd have found it by now?" Eric scoffed, shaking his head. "But hey, if you wanna go off and play savior, be my guest. Just remember – you walk away, you're on your own."

"Is that a threat?" Jason asked, his voice cold.

"Call it what you want," Eric replied, his eyes hardening. "I'm just telling you how it is."

With that, Eric turned and walked away, leaving Jason to grapple with his decision alone. As he stood in the moonlit silence, Jason knew that the choice before him would define not only his future but also the lives of those around him. The weight of responsibility felt crushing, suffocating.

As he stared into the darkness, the sirens and barking dogs fading into the background, one question haunted him: could he truly walk away from this family he had become a part of? Or was he destined to remain trapped in this cycle of violence, forever bound to the gang that had become his family?

The answer remained as elusive as the shadows that enveloped him, leaving Jason to wrestle with his doubts and fears as the night wore on.

5

Trouble In Paradise

The Friday evening air was balmy and thick through the streets of the small town. Jason had taken a job at a restaurant to make more money and support the new members of his household. It had been a week since the girls had been welcomed into their new home, but they had been adjusting well to school and seemed to be in good spirits. Despite the girls being away from the gang all week, they had asked if they could go to the party house that night to see everyone. At first, Jason hesitated, but he just couldn't deny his little ones the opportunity of seeing their friends once more. As they drove, Jason could almost feel the anticipation in the truck. He had grown to love these girls during his time with them, and he wanted only the best for them. He could sense the excitement as they pulled up to the same spot they always frequented and quickly made their way to the party house. The door was opened by Cynthia, who welcomed them in with wide arms. Inside, there were hugs and laughter as the girls were reunited with their friends, and Jason couldn't help but feel at ease. He stood watching in the background, feeling a sense of contentment wash over him as he watched the joy of the reunion.

Jason, fraught with dilemma, leaned against a wall, staring into the distance as his heart raced with conflicting emotions. He knew he couldn't abandon Rachel, Consuelo, and Calisto, but what could he do? The gang had become his family, giving him a sense of belonging that he had never experienced before.

"Yo, J!" called out Tom, snapping Jason out of his thoughts. "You alright, man?"

Jason nodded. "Yeah, I'm good," he replied, forcing a smile. But inside, he felt anything but good. The weight of his decision pressed down on him like a ton of bricks.

"Look, man," Tom said, clapping a hand on Jason's shoulder. "I know things have been crazy lately, but we got your back no matter what."

Jason looked into Tom's eyes, searching for reassurance. He knew that staying in the gang was dangerous, but at the same time, he couldn't leave the girls to fend for themselves. They needed protection from the harsh realities of the streets, and he was the only one who could provide it.

"Thanks, Tom," he said finally, his voice wavering with emotion. "I'm not going anywhere. I just... I need to make sure the girls are safe too."

"Understood," Tom replied, nodding solemnly. "We'll all look out for them. That's what family does, right?"

"Right," Jason agreed, swallowing hard. He knew he was making a risky choice, but he couldn't see any other way forward. With a deep breath, he pushed away from the wall and joined the rest of the gang, his resolve solidifying with each step.

As the days turned into weeks, Jason worked tirelessly to ensure the safety of Rachel, Consuelo and Calisto. Jason drove them to school every day, brought them home in the afternoons, and spent countless hours teaching them how to defend themselves against any potential threats.

"Remember," he told them one afternoon as they practiced their punches on a worn punching bag, "you need to be strong, but you also need to be smart. Don't go looking for trouble, but if it finds you, be ready to fight back."

Rachel, Consuelo and Calisto nodded, their eyes shining with determination. They understood the gravity of their situation, and they were grateful for Jason's unwavering support.

"Thanks for everything, Jason," Calisto whispered to him one night as they lay in bed, her hand resting gently on his chest. "I don't know what we would do without you."

"Me neither," Jason admitted, his heart aching with love for her and the other girls. "But I promise I'll always be here for you, no matter what."

And as they drifted off to sleep, entwined in each other's arms, Jason knew that he had made the right choice. Protecting the ones he loved was worth any risk, no matter how great.

The next afternoon, Jason stood on the balcony of his apartment, watching Calisto study at the small table inside. Her brow furrowed in concentration, she occasionally bit her lip as she worked through her math problems. He felt a swell of pride for her dedication, and a fierce love that only seemed to intensify with every passing day.

"Jason," Calisto called softly, interrupting his thoughts. "Can you help me with this one?"

"Of course," he replied, stepping back into the apartment. Sitting down beside her, he wrapped an arm around her shoulders and began explaining the equation. She leaned against him, her body warm and comforting.

"Thanks," she murmured when they finished, pressing a soft kiss to his cheek.

"You're really good at this."

"Anything for you," he whispered, squeezing her hand.

In the living room, Rachel and Consuelo were sprawled across the floor, textbooks open around them. Their focus had improved tremendously since they stopped drinking and using drugs, but it hadn't been easy. There were moments when temptation threatened to consume them, but Jason's unwavering support kept them grounded.

"Rach, I think I've got this English assignment figured out," Consuelo said triumphantly, her eyes lighting up as she shared her interpretation of the text.

"Nice job!" Rachel praised, grinning at her friend. "Jason, see? We're getting better!"

"I'm proud of you both," Jason told them sincerely, feeling a surge of hope for their futures.

Later that night, after the girls had gone to bed, Jason and Calisto sat on the balcony, holding hands loosely. The stars above twinkled brightly, casting a gentle light upon their faces.

"Calisto," Jason began, his voice cracking with emotion. "I never thought I could feel this way about someone. You've changed my life, and I can't imagine a future without you."

"Jason," she whispered, tears glistening in her eyes. "I love you so much. You make me feel safe and loved, even when everything else is falling apart."

"Promise me," he implored, his voice barely audible. "Promise me we'll face whatever comes our way together."

"I promise," Calisto vowed, their fingers tightening around each other's. "Together, always."

Jason pulled a gleaming black hills gold diamond ring from his pocket and proffered it to Calisto with a smile. "We may be young," he said, "but I've never felt love as strong as this before. The only way I can continue to feel this way is if we're together forever. Will you marry me?"

Calisto, eyes wide, was momentarily speechless. Tears suddenly streamed down her face and she held out her hand for him to place the ring on her finger. "Yes Jason, yes!" she cried, overcome with emotion.

Their love continued to grow stronger, a beacon of hope amidst the chaos of their lives. And as they faced the challenges that lay ahead, Jason knew they would never give up on each other, no matter the cost.

Weeks had passed since that night on the balcony, when Jason and Calisto vowed to face their challenges together. Life within the gang had settled into an uneasy calm, a fragile harmony that everyone seemed to cherish. The afternoons spent studying with Rachel, Calisto and Consuelo had become routine, and the girls' progress in their studies brought Jason a sense of pride and hope.

One sunny afternoon, Jason drove through the city streets with Rachel, Calisto, and Consuelo by his side. They chatted animatedly about their upcoming exams and exchanged jokes, laughter filling the car.

"Hey, I got one!" Rachel announced. "What do you call a pig who knows karate?"

"Uh, I don't know. What?" Consuelo asked curiously.

"A Pork Chop!" Rachel burst out laughing, and the others followed suit, momentarily forgetting the harsh reality of their lives.

As they pulled up to a red light, Jason's eyes caught sight of a familiar van approaching from the opposite lane. His heart rate quickened, and his grip on the steering wheel tightened. It was the same van that belonged to the rival gang who had invited them to the hotel party weeks ago. He could see the faces of the members inside, their expressions cold and menacing.

"Jason? What's wrong?" Calisto asked, sensing his sudden tension. He didn't have time to answer before the van's door slid open, revealing a figure holding a shotgun, aimed directly at him.

"Get down!" Jason shouted, slamming his foot on the accelerator as the girls screamed and ducked, covering their heads with their arms.

"Jason, what's happening?!" Rachel cried, her voice trembling with fear.

"Rival gang," he muttered through gritted teeth, his focus solely on the road ahead as he swerved the wrong way onto a one-way street, adrenaline pumping through his veins. The chase ensued, tires screeching and engine roaring as both vehicles sped through the city streets, weaving in and out of on-coming traffic.

"Jason, please, get us out of here!" Calisto pleaded, her eyes filled with tears as she clutched onto his arm.

"Trust me, Calisto," Jason replied, his mind racing to find a way to evade their pursuers. "I'm trying!"

As they rounded another corner, he spotted an alleyway just wide enough for their truck. He turned sharply into it, praying that the rivals wouldn't follow. They didn't. After several more twists and turns, the sound of the van's engine faded, leaving only the pounding of Jason's heart and the ragged breaths of the girls.

"Are they gone?" Consuelo asked, her voice barely audible.

"Looks like it," Jason replied, trying to calm his own nerves. "We're safe now, but we can't let our guard down."

"Jason, thank you," Calisto whispered, her fingers trembling as they intertwined with his. In that instant, Jason vowed to safeguard Calisto and the young ladies from any peril regardless of the risks involved. He was willing to go to any lengths for their safety, even if it meant putting his own life on the line.

As the engine hummed to a stop, Jason looked around, making sure they were truly safe. His heart thudded in his chest, the adrenaline still coursing through his veins. Finally, he allowed himself a shaky breath, realizing that the chase was over.

"Is everyone okay?" He asked, concern lacing his voice.

Rachel nodded, her eyes wide, but her expression determined. "Yeah, we're fine."

Consuelo and Calisto echoed their agreement, although Calisto's grip on Jason's hand tightened as she spoke. The fear in her eyes was evident but so was the trust she had placed in him.

"Let's get out of here," Jason suggested, pulling the truck back onto the road. As they drove, the conversation between them was cautious at first, each of them processing the events that had just unfolded.

"Jason, how'd you know that alley would be there?" Rachel inquired, her curiosity piqued.

"Actually, I didn't," he admitted, gripping the steering wheel tightly. "I just took a chance, and it paid off."

"Next time, let's try not to need any chances," Consuelo muttered, rubbing her arms as if she could wipe away the goosebumps that still lingered.

"Agreed," Jason replied, guiding the truck towards home. Inwardly, he knew that this close call wouldn't be their last. He wondered how long he could keep up this balancing act – protecting the girls while remaining in the gang. But for now, all he could do was focus on getting them home safely.

Weeks went by without incident, and life seemed to return to normal. However, the respite was short-lived. One morning, police officers showed up at Jason's door, armed with a warrant for his arrest. Accused of harboring runaways, specifically Rachel, Consuelo, and Calisto, he was handcuffed and led away while the girls were forcibly returned to their homes.

"Jason!" Calisto cried out as she watched him being led away. "You can't take him!"

"Please," Rachel pleaded, her voice breaking. "He's just trying to help us."

The officers were unmoved, and Jason could only offer a reassuring smile as he was loaded into the squad car. "It'll be okay," he called out to them, his voice heavy with grief. "Just take care of each other."

For thirty long days, Jason languished in jail, his thoughts constantly turning to the girls and wondering how they were coping without him. He wondered if they would still be waiting for him when he was released. And most of all, he worried about Calisto – her safety, her well-being, and the future that awaited them both.

The heavy iron door creaked open before Jason, sunlight streaming through the gaps like a beacon of hope. He took his first steps out of jail, blinking against the brightness, the air outside tasting like freedom on his tongue. It had been thirty days since he'd seen the girls, and he wondered what awaited him now.

When he reached his apartment, his heart stuttered in his chest as he found Rachel waiting for him on the front stoop, her eyes red-rimmed from crying. "Jason!" she cried, launching herself into his arms. "We missed you so much!"

"Rachel," he said softly, hugging her back. "What about Calisto? How is she?"

"Come inside," Rachel urged, leading him into the dimly lit space that he used to call home. There, he found Calisto sitting on the floor, her knees drawn up to her chest, her dark eyes wide with relief as they met his own.

"Calisto," he breathed, sinking down beside her. "You're here."

"Of course I'm here," she replied fiercely, throwing her arms around him. "I couldn't stay away. We both ran away again, couldn't stand living without you, without each other."

As he held her close, Jason could feel the warmth of her body against his, the steady rhythm of her heartbeat. In that moment, he realized just how deeply his feelings for Calisto had grown. She was more than just a teenage infatuation – she was a part of him now, entwined with his very soul.

"Calisto," he whispered, pulling back to look at her. "I don't want to give this up. Us. Our relationship. I'll do whatever it takes to keep us together."

"Me too," she murmured, her eyes shining with determination. "We'll face whatever comes, as long as we're together."

"Promise me," Jason insisted, his voice thick with emotion. "Promise me that no matter what, we'll stand by each other, support each other through the challenges that lie ahead."

"I promise," Calisto vowed, her hand slipping into his. And as their fingers intertwined, a spark of hope lit up the darkness in Jason's heart.

Together, they would face whatever life threw at them – the gang, the police, the hardships of living on the run. For now, though, they had each other, and that was enough to keep them moving forward, one step at a time.

As Jason and Calisto stood together in the dim light of the apartment, a sense of unity washed over them. They knew that the road ahead would be fraught with danger and uncertainty, but they were determined to face it together.

"Jason," Calisto said softly, her voice wavering slightly as she stared into his eyes. "I'm scared of what's going to happen next."

"Me too," he admitted, his own voice barely above a whisper. "But we'll figure it out. We have each other, and that's what matters."

The apartment was quiet, save for the distant sound of sirens wailing outside. Despite the calmness within, Jason couldn't shake the feeling that they were standing on the edge of an abyss, teetering between safety and disaster. He knew that their lives had changed irrevocably the moment they chose to stay together, and there was no turning back.

"Let's make a plan," Rachel suggested, breaking the silence. She had been sitting on the couch, watching the exchange between the couple with a mixture of worry and hope. "We can't just wing it anymore. Things are different now."

"Right," Calisto agreed, nodding. "We need to be smart about this if we're going to make it work."

"Okay," Jason said, taking a deep breath and glancing around at the small group gathered in his apartment. "First things first – we need to lay low for a while. The rival gang will be after us, not to mention the police."

"And us girls should find a way to make some money," Calisto added, her brow furrowed in thought. "We can't keep relying on your working, handouts from friends and stealing."

"Agreed," Jason said. "Maybe you can find some odd jobs or something. And we'll need to be careful not to draw attention to ourselves."

"Sounds like a plan," Rachel said with determination, her eyes meeting Jason's. "We'll do whatever it takes to stay together and stay out of trouble."

"Exactly," Calisto chimed in, her voice filled with resolve. "We're in this together, no matter what."

As they began devising their plan for the future, Jason felt a strange mix of fear and excitement churning within him. He knew that the challenges ahead would test them in ways they couldn't yet imagine. But he also knew that as long as they had each other, they stood a chance.

With each passing day, it became increasingly clear that the life they once knew was slipping further and further away. But in its place, a new path was taking shape – one full of risk and uncertainty, but also hope and love. And as they prepared to take the first steps down that road, Jason couldn't help but feel that maybe – just maybe – they could find a way to make it through the storm together.

6

The Breaking Point

The past few months had been a whirlwind of violence, friendship ,romance, and a constant struggle for survival. Jason found himself questioning the path he had chosen, his once unwavering loyalty to the gang now wavering. The bloodshed, the sense of always looking over his shoulder, and the realization that the gang offered little in the way of a future had begun to gnaw at the edges of his commitment. The glitz and glamour had faded, leaving only a sickening feeling in the pit of his stomach.

One evening, as Jason brooded in silence on the worn couch of their cramped apartment, a knock at the door shattered the room's tense atmosphere. Rachel, her face etched with concern, cautiously opened the door to reveal Consuelo, bags in hand and eyes red from tears.

"Consuelo?" Jason asked, his voice filled with surprise. "What are you doing here?"

"I… I can't take it anymore," she whispered, her voice trembling. "I had to run away."

"Come in," Rachel said softly, pulling her inside. "We'll figure something out."

As Consuelo settled into the small living space, Jason couldn't help but feel a twinge of guilt. He knew all too well the price of running away from home and the dangers they now faced as a group. But he also knew that turning her away was not an option; they were family, bound by shared experiences and the desperate need for something better than the life they had known.

"Are you okay?" Calisto asked Consuelo, her eyes filled with worry.

"Y-yeah," she stammered. "I just couldn't stay there any longer. It was suffocating."

Jason exchanged a glance with Rachel before turning his attention back to Consuelo. He understood her pain and the desire for freedom, but he also recognized the risk they were taking in harboring her. The gang would not look kindly on the fact that one of their own had chosen to leave and seek refuge with a disenchanted former member.

"Listen," he began, his voice low and serious. "You're welcome here, but we have to be careful. If anyone finds out you're staying with us, we could all be in danger."

"I know," she nodded, fear in her eyes. "I'll do my best to stay out of sight."

"Good," Jason said, a hint of resolve returning to his voice. "We'll make this work. Somehow."

As the four of them sat in their incommodious living room, each lost in thought, Jason couldn't help but feel that the fragile peace they had managed to carve out for themselves was about to be shattered. Yet despite the looming threat, he found solace in the knowledge that they were together, bound by a shared determination to turn their backs on the destructive path they had once embraced.

The next evening, Jason returned from work, his hands felt greasy from the hours spent flipping burgers, and the smell of frying oil clung to his clothes. His new job at the fast food joint was a far cry from what he had been used to, and the pay barely covered their necessities. It was a constant reminder of how far he had fallen since his arrest. The gang life seemed like a distant memory, but its consequences continued to haunt him.

"Hey Jason," Rachel said, entering the small apartment with Consuelo in tow. "We got something for dinner."

The girls held up plastic bags filled with groceries as they grinned sheepishly. Jason could see the excitement on their faces, an excitement that gnawed at him. He knew they hadn't purchased those groceries; they'd stolen them.

"Are you guys serious?" Jason asked, trying to mask his concern with anger. "You can't just go around stealing stuff."

"Look, we're just trying to help out," Rachel shot back, her voice defensive. "We need this stuff, and it's not like we can afford it."

As much as he hated to admit it, she was right. They were all struggling to make ends meet, and the temptation to resort to crime was overwhelming. But Jason couldn't bear the thought of Rachel and Consuelo getting into trouble.

"Listen," he began, looking both girls in the eyes. "I appreciate the effort, I really do. But this isn't the way. We've come too far to go back to that life."

Rachel sighed, shifting her weight from one foot to another. "So what are we supposed to do? Starve?"

"Maybe we can find another way," Jason suggested, feeling his resolve wavering. "Calisto could look for a job, or I could try to pick up more shifts."

"Jason, we're just kids," Consuelo interjected quietly. "We don't have a lot of options."

He knew she was right, but the thought of watching these girls fall back into old habits broke his heart. He didn't want them to suffer, but he couldn't condone their actions either.

"Promise me you won't do this again," he pleaded, his voice barely above a whisper. "Please."

Rachel hesitated for a moment before nodding reluctantly. "Fine. We promise."

"Good," Jason said, trying to sound firm even as he felt a cold knot of anxiety tightening in his chest. They were trapped in a vicious cycle, and he worried that their determination to escape it would only lead them deeper into danger.

As they sat down to eat their ill-gotten meal, Jason was overwhelmed by a sense of impending doom, as if they were standing on the brink of disaster. And as much as he tried to pull them back from the brink, he feared that he wouldn't be strong enough to save them from themselves.

The days blurred together as Jason struggled to keep his life from spinning out of control. At the fast food joint, he worked tirelessly, trying to make ends meet while the tension at home grew thicker by the minute. He could feel the distance growing between him and his friends – Ryan, Tom, Eric, and John. Once inseparable, they now seemed like strangers occupying different worlds.

"Hey, man, you coming to the party tonight?" Tom asked one afternoon, leaning against the wall outside the break room, his eyes shadowed with concern.

Jason hesitated, wiping the sweat from his brow. "I don't know," he replied, glancing back towards the kitchen where he was supposed to be working. "I've got a lot going on right now."

"Look, I get it," Tom said, his voice softening. "But you can't just shut us out. We're still your friends, cuz."

"Are you?" Jason snapped, surprising himself with the bitterness in his tone. "Because all I see is a bunch of guys who don't understand what I'm going through."

"Maybe we would if you'd talk to us," Tom countered, hurt flashing across his face before he turned and walked away.

That night, as the chill of the fall air settled in, Jason found himself standing outside Rachel's house, heart pounding in his chest. Calisto stood beside him, her hand warm and reassuring in his, while Rachel and Consuelo huddled together, whispering nervously.

"Are you sure she's gone?" Jason asked Rachel, scanning the darkened windows for any sign of movement.

"Positive," Rachel replied, her voice tight with determination. "She's at some stupid work event. We've got maybe an hour, tops."

"Let's do this then," Calisto whispered, her grip on Jason's hand tightening.

They moved quickly and quietly, slipping through the shadows like ghosts as they made their way to the back door. Rachel produced a key, her hands shaking slightly as she fumbled with the lock.

"Got it," she hissed, pushing the door open just wide enough for them to slip inside.

The house was eerily silent, each creaking floorboard and labored breath echoing like a gunshot in the darkness. Jason followed Calisto and the others up the stairs, his heart hammering against his ribcage as they crept towards Rachel's room.

"Grab what you need and let's get out of here," he whispered, watching as Rachel pulled open her closet and began rifling through the clothes hanging there.

"Jason," Calisto murmured, touching his arm gently. "Are you okay?"

He stared at her, the fear in her eyes mirroring his own, and suddenly felt an overwhelming surge of love and desperation. It was all too much – the strain of keeping his friends close while trying to protect these girls who had come to mean so much to him. And now here they were, breaking into a house like common criminals.

"Let's just get this over with," he replied, forcing a weak smile onto his face.

The moon hung low in the sky, casting its silvery light across the streets as Jason navigated the truck through the familiar roads of their neighborhood. He could sense the tension in the air; the girls were huddled together , clutching Rachel's hastily-packed bags to their chests like lifelines. It felt like a fuse had been lit, and Jason couldn't help but wonder how long they had before everything blew up.

"Is everyone okay?" he asked, glancing sideways to catch a glimpse of their faces.

"Fine," Rachel muttered, her voice tight with unspoken worry. Consuelo nodded, her dark eyes wide and fearful, while Calisto bit her lip, her knuckles white from gripping the fabric of her seat.

"Jason…" Calisto trailed off, swallowing hard before continuing. "What if we get caught?"

He didn't respond immediately, his thoughts racing alongside the truck's tires as they sped down the street. The truth was, he wasn't sure what would happen if they got caught. It seemed like life had become an endless maze of consequences, each decision leading to another dead end or trap.

"Let's just focus on getting back to Cynthia's house," he said finally, trying to sound reassuring. "We can figure everything out from there."

They pulled up to the party house, its windows black and vacant like hollowed-out eyes. As Jason parked the truck, he noticed that the street seemed unnaturally quiet, the shadows stretching out like long, grasping fingers. A chill ran down his spine, and he suddenly felt exposed, vulnerable.

"Stay in the truck," he whispered to the girls, his instincts screaming at him to be cautious. "I'll go check it out."

As he approached the front door, he couldn't shake the feeling that something was wrong. Every step seemed to echo in the stillness, and he found himself holding his breath, waiting for some unknown threat to materialize.

"Jason!" Calisto's urgent whisper broke through the silence, and he turned to see her running towards him, panic etched across her face. "There's someone in the backyard!"

"Who?" he demanded, instantly on high alert.

"Police," she choked out, fear making her voice tremble. "I saw them through the fence."

"Damn it!" Jason cursed under his breath, the weight of reality crashing down on him like a tidal wave. They were cornered, and there was no way out.

"Get back in the truck," he ordered, his mind racing as he tried to come up with a plan. "We'll figure something out."

But as they piled into the vehicle, the sound of sirens filled the air, their wailing cries echoing through the night like harbingers of doom. Blue and red lights illuminated the street, casting eerie shadows as the police cars pulled up, boxing them in.

"Hands up!" a voice barked from behind them, and Jason felt a cold sweat break out on his forehead. This was it; the end of the line.

"Jason..." Calisto whispered, her eyes pleading with him to find a solution, but he knew there was nothing left to do.

"Whatever happens," he murmured, his heart heavy with regret, "just know that I love you all and I tried my best."

As the officers approached, weapons drawn, Jason raised his hands in surrender, his thoughts consumed by the grim realization that this was just the beginning of a long and treacherous path.

The sudden flash of red and blue lights bathed the truck's interior in a kaleidoscope of ominous hues, casting distorted shadows that mirrored Jason's inner turmoil. His heart pounded in his chest, each beat a frantic plea for escape as he felt the weight of the situation crushing him. Around him, Rachel, Calisto, and Consuelo sat frozen with fear, their eyes wide and unblinking.

"Everyone out of the truck! Now!" The commanding voice of an officer cut through the tension like a knife. Jason's hands, slick with sweat, clenched the steering wheel tightly as he fought the urge to flee. But he knew it was futile;

they were trapped.

"Let's go. Slow and steady," he whispered, forcing himself to swallow the panic threatening to overwhelm him. One by one, they stepped out of the vehicle, hands raised in submission. Their breaths were shallow and uneven, punctuated by the distant howls of sirens.

"Get down on your knees!" another officer barked, his gun trained on them with unwavering focus. As they complied, Jason caught sight of Rachel's mother standing nearby, her face twisted in a visage of anger and betrayal.

"Is this what you wanted?" Jason thought bitterly, feeling a surge of resentment towards her. "To see us cuffed and humiliated? To tear us apart?"

"Officer, they broke into my house and threatened me with a gun!" Rachel's mother cried, her voice quivering with indignation. The accusation sent a jolt of disbelief through Jason, who couldn't fathom why she would resort to such a lie.

"Ma'am, we're going to investigate these claims thoroughly," the officer assured her, his voice stern but professional. "For now, we need everyone to remain calm."

As Jason knelt on the cold pavement, the handcuffs biting into his wrists, he couldn't help but feel a sense of despair creeping in. The taste of metallic fear lingered on his tongue as he silently prayed for a miracle.

"Jason," Calisto whispered, her voice barely audible over the thrum of adrenaline coursing through his veins. "We didn't do it. They'll see that, right?"

"I hope so," he replied, his voice laced with uncertainty. He knew that even if they were cleared of the false accusations, the damage had been done. Trust had been shattered, and the delicate balance of their makeshift family was now nearing the edge of collapse.

"Please let this be over soon," he thought, his inner plea drowned out by the racket of sirens, shouting, and the unrelenting flurry of images that threatened to consume him. His eyes locked onto Rachel's, and in that moment of shared anguish, he realized just how much they all stood to lose.

The officers eventually uncuffed Jason, a dull ache lingering in his wrists as he rubbed them. "You're free to go, kid," one officer informed him with a curt nod. "We didn't find any evidence that supports the allegations. But we still need to take the girls back to their homes."

"Wait, you can't do that!" Rachel protested, her eyes wide with fear. "You have no idea what our home life is like!"

"Sorry, but that's not up to us," the officer replied, his tone firm and unwavering.

Jason felt a surge of helplessness wash over him as he watched Calisto and Rachel being escorted into separate squad cars, their faces etched with despair.

"Take care of yourself, Jason," Consuelo whispered tearfully before she was guided away into her house. Her words stung, a painful reminder of the consequences of their choices.

"Please, just let me say goodbye," Jason pleaded with the officer, his voice strained with emotion.

"Make it quick," the officer replied, relenting for a brief moment.

He approached Rachel, their hands reaching out to touch through the cold metal bars of the squad car window. "I'm sorry, Rach. I'll figure something out, I promise."

"Be careful, Jay," she whispered, her fingers trembling against his. "I love you."

"I love you too," he choked out, forcing a smile onto his face even as his heart splintered within his chest.

Jason walked slowly towards the police car that was holding Calisto, his throat tightening with every step. He knew what awaited her when she got home—the judgment, the disappointment, the fear—and it tore him apart to know that he had put her in such a vulnerable position. He stopped beside the vehicle, his lips trembling as he fought back tears. Calisto weakly pushed open the door and stepped out, her eyes filling with despair as they met his. "I'm sorry," he croaked out, words falling short of conveying the depths of his anguish. "It's okay," she whispered back, her voice barely audible over the sound of sirens in the night sky. She stepped into his arms and held him tightly, time standing still as they clung onto each other for dear life. "We'll see each other again," Jason promised softly as they parted ways, knowing deep down that there were no guarantees in life. He watched until Calisto's car disappeared into the horizon before turning away to begin picking up the shattered pieces of their lives one by one.

As the police cars pulled away, their red and blue lights slicing through the darkness, Jason stood alone in the night. He could feel the weight of his decisions pressing down upon him like an unbearable burden. The gang life had led him here, to this desolate crossroads where the people he cared about most were ripped away from him.

"Is this really worth it?" he thought, his breath visible in the crisp night air. "How many more nights like this are we going to face if we continue down this path?"

As the sirens faded into the distance, Jason knew he had a choice to make –

one that would define not only his future but the fates of those he held closest to his heart. A decision that could either save them or condemn them to a life of fear and uncertainty.

With a heavy heart, Jason climbed back into his truck, the empty seats a stark reminder of the loved ones who were no longer beside him. The engine roared to life as he gripped the steering wheel, determined to forge a new path for himself and those he cared for most. As he entered his apartment, Jason collapsed on the couch, his entire body trembling from the events of the night. He had never felt more alone in his life. His apartment was empty and silent, devoid of any trace of life or warmth. The only thing that kept him company were his thoughts—dark and oppressive memories of a world he'd tried so hard to leave behind.

7

A Way Out

T he days had turned cold as winter drew near. Snow covered the ground and the temperature had dropped to only single digits outside. A few days had passed since the police incident, but Calisto, Rachel, and Consuelo were still grappling with the aftermath. Though they had tried to return to some semblance of normalcy, the shadows of fear and uncertainty continued to hover over them like a dark cloud.

"Hey, Calisto, pass me the soda," Rachel called out, trying to lighten the mood. She sat cross-legged on the floor of Calisto's bedroom, her demure frame wrapped in a worn-out hoodie. Despite her best efforts to hide it, her eyes betrayed a deep concern for their current situation.

"Here," Calisto replied, tossing the bottle towards Rachel. Her islander features, once a beacon of light and laughter, now appeared weary and guarded. The weight of the past few days seemed to have aged her beyond her now 16 years.

Consuelo sat silently on the corner of the bed. At only 14 years old, she had always looked up to her big sister Cynthia and her friends, eager to be a part of their world. Now, however, she found herself wishing for simpler times, when such dangerous consequences had been far from her mind.

As the three girls sat together in the fading light, their thoughts turned inevitably to Jason – the boy who had risked everything to protect them, only to find himself more alone than ever before.

Jason wandered the streets aimlessly, his heart heavy with despair. The events of the past few days had left him feeling like a ghost, haunting the edges of his old life but unable to truly connect with it. His tall, skinny frame seemed to shrink under the burden of his sorrow, and his once-gleaming blue eyes were now dull and lifeless.

"Hey, man, you good?" a familiar voice called out, causing Jason to look up. It was Kathy, one of his friends from the gang, concern etched on her face as she took in Jason's disheveled appearance. Deep down, Jason knew that his friends could offer little solace for the pain he was feeling, but he couldn't help but wish that they could somehow make everything right again.

"Hey," Jason replied, forcing a weak smile onto his face. "Yeah, I'm alright." But even as the words left his mouth, he knew that he was far from alright. In fact, he had never felt more alone or lost in his entire life. All he could think about were Calisto, Rachel, and Consuelo – the girls who had come to mean so much to him, now facing their own struggles as a result of the choices he had made.

As the sun set, twilight descended and the city was cloaked in shadows. Jason continued to wander aimlessly, searching for some semblance of hope in the desolate landscape of his heart.

Days turned into nights as the city continued to buzz with life, indifferent to the turmoil brewing within Jason. He had quit his job, unable to focus on anything but his fading existence. The image of the girls' tear-streaked faces as the police took them away haunted his every waking moment.

"Man, I can't take this anymore," Jason muttered to himself, his restlessness pushing him to seek solace from the only other place he felt he belonged – Cynthia's house, where his gang friends often gathered.

He approached the familiar door, a sense of blissfulness washing over him despite the heavy weight in his chest. The sounds of laughter and video games greeted him as he walked inside, the dimly lit room filled with familiar faces. He was met with hearty pats on the back and knowing smirks, but none of it could truly lift his spirits.

"Hey, Jay, you made it!" Cynthia shouted over the sounds blaring from the television, her long black hair swaying as she moved towards him. Her eyes betrayed a hint of concern, but it was quickly masked by her party girl persona. "How've you been?"

"Been better, Cyn," Jason replied, forcing a smile that didn't quite reach his eyes. "Just needed a break from everything, you know?"

"Totally get it," Cynthia nodded, handing him a beer. "You'll always have a place here with us."

As Jason sipped his drink, he couldn't help but feel a pang of guilt for seeking comfort in the very lifestyle that had cost him his relationship with Calisto, Rachel, and Consuelo. But what else could he do? They were all he had left.

"Yo, J! Come play pool with us," one of his gang friends called out, breaking Jason's train of thought. He hesitated for a moment, wondering if he should indulge in the distraction or continue to wallow in misery.

"Go on, Jason," Cynthia encouraged him gently. "It'll do you good to get your mind off things for a while."

"Alright," he relented, setting his beer down and joining his friends at the pool table. As they laughed and joked around, Jason's thoughts kept drifting back to the girls – their smiles, their laughter, and the warmth they brought into his life. He wished with all his heart that he could turn back time and make different choices, but reality was harsh and unforgiving.

"Jason, you're up," his friend nudged him, bringing him back to the present moment. He took a deep breath, steadied his hand, and aimed the cue, secretly hoping that the perfect shot would somehow make everything right again.

"Nice one, man!" his friend exclaimed as the ball rolled smoothly into the pocket. But despite the praise and jocularity surrounding him, Jason knew deep down that this false sense of belonging was nothing compared to the love and connection he had shared with the three girls. And so, with every victorious shot and cheer from his gang friends, Jason's heart continued to ache for what he had lost.

Jason stepped away from the pool table, feeling the weight of his thoughts pulling him down. He glanced around the room, his gaze landing on Jackie sitting in a corner, her two little boys Jessie and Johnnie playing by her feet.

"Hey, Jackie," he called out, his voice barely audible over the clamor of laughter and music. She looked up, a tired smile spreading across her face as she beckoned him over. Jason settled down next to her, watching the boys with a mix of affection and concern.

"Jackie, I've been thinking…" he began hesitantly, his eyes still fixed on the kids. "About all of us – me, you, Cynthia, Consuelo – and how we're living our lives."

She tilted her head slightly, her expression one of curiosity and caution. "What about it?"

"Look at your boys," Jason implored, gesturing towards the two children who were now wrestling on the floor. "They deserve better than this, Jackie. All of us do."

Jackie sighed, her shoulders slumping as she took in the scene before her. "I know, Jason. But what can we do? This is the life we were born into."

"Change," he said simply, his conviction clear in his voice. "For them, for Cynthia, for Consuelo... we need to break free from this life."

A moment of silence passed between them, broken only by the playful shouts of Jessie and Johnnie. Finally, Jackie spoke up, her voice trembling. "It's not easy, Jason. You know that."

"I do," he agreed, his heart heavy with the knowledge of just how difficult it would be. "But we've got to try, Jackie. For their sake."

"Alright," she murmured, her resolve slowly taking shape. "I'll do my best."

"Thank you," Jason whispered, placing a hand on her shoulder in gratitude and support. Just then, Cynthia approached, her eyes filled with worry.

"Jason, I've got some news," she said hesitantly, glancing at Jackie before continuing. "Rachel and Calisto – they were forced to drop out of the school you got them into. They're struggling in their new schools, and it's tearing them apart."

The anguish in Jason's heart intensified upon hearing this revelation. He closed his eyes, trying to block out the world around him for a moment. The thought of those he loved suffering only served to strengthen his resolve.

"Jackie," he said, turning back to face her, his voice filled with determination. "We need to do this – not just for your boys, but for all of us. We can't let our past define our future."

"Okay," Jackie agreed, her own resolve hardening. "We'll find a way, Jason. Together."

"Promise?" he asked, extending his pinky finger towards her.

"Promise," she replied, linking her pinky with his. Their intertwined fingers stood as a symbol of hope – a hope that, against all odds, they would find a way to break free from the chains of street life and build a better future for themselves and their loved ones.

The moon cast a silvery glow on the empty streets, as Jason stood leaning against the wall of an old building. He shivered slightly in the cold night air but refused to let his impatience show. It had been nearly a month since he had seen Calisto, Rachel, and Consuelo, and though it felt like an eternity, he knew they were taking a risk by sneaking out to meet him.

"Jason!" The sudden whisper startled him, and he turned to see Calisto, her dark eyes filled with excitement and fear. Rachel and Consuelo followed closely behind, their faces flushed from adrenaline.

"Hey," he breathed, relief flooding through him at the sight of them. "I've missed you guys so much."

"Same here," Rachel replied, her gap-toothed grin lighting up her beautiful freckled face. "Feels like forever."

"Come on," Jason said, leading them away from the dimly lit street corner. "I've got something planned for us tonight."

As they walked, Jason couldn't help but notice the changes in the girls. They seemed more guarded, their shoulders tense and their gazes constantly scanning their surroundings. It angered him to see them like this, struggling to adapt after being forced to drop out of their schools. He clenched his fists, vowing to find a way to make things right.

"Where are we going?" Consuelo asked, her curiosity momentarily overshadowing her anxiety.

"Somewhere fun," Jason replied, a mischievous glint in his blue eyes. "You'll see."

A short while later, they arrived at an unassuming building in the heart of downtown. The neon sign above the entrance read 'Laser Tag', casting a vibrant glow across the sidewalk. "It's not much," Jason said, rubbing the back of his neck, "But I thought it'd be a good way for us to blow off some steam."

"Jason, this is perfect," Calisto said, her eyes shining as she took in the flashing lights inside. "We really needed this." He could tell by the sincerity in her voice that she truly appreciated his effort to lift their spirits.

"Alright, let's do this!" Rachel exclaimed, her enthusiasm contagious as they all eagerly entered the building.

Inside the laser tag arena, the four of them were transported into a futuristic world filled with neon lights and adrenaline-pumping music. The weight of reality seemed to temporarily lift from their shoulders as they darted through the maze-like corridors, laughing and shouting tactical commands to one another.

"Rach, cover me! I'm going for the flag!" Jason called out, ducking behind a glowing barrier.

"Got your back!" she responded, taking aim at an opposing player and firing a well-placed shot. As they played, Jason found himself lost in the moment, reveling in the fierce competition and friendship that had been missing from his life in recent weeks.

"Guys, we make a great team," Consuelo said, grinning after they emerged victorious from yet another game.

"Always have, always will," Calisto added, reaching out to squeeze Jason's hand. He felt a warmth spread through him at her touch, a feeling of belonging that he hadn't realized he'd been craving so desperately.

But amid the laughter and excitement, Jason couldn't shake the nagging realization that this moment was just a fleeting escape from the harsh realities waiting outside. They couldn't hide behind the neon lights forever, and soon enough, they would have to face the consequences of their actions – both past and present. For now, though, he would savor the joy of being together, united against the world if only for a brief instant.

As the group exited the laser tag arena, their laughter and adrenaline still coursing through their veins, Jason noticed the flashing blue and red lights reflecting off the puddles in the parking lot. His heartbeat quickened, and he instinctively tightened his grip on Calisto's hand. The sound of hurried footsteps and authoritative voices cut through the night air like a knife.

"Jason!" Calisto gasped, her eyes wide with fear. "What are we going to do?"

"Stay calm," he whispered, trying to keep his own panic at bay. "Let me handle this."

The police closed in, their stern expressions leaving no doubt as to the seriousness of the situation. A woman stepped forward, her tough, rugged features illuminated by the swirling lights. Officer Sue – notorious for her no-nonsense attitude and unwavering commitment to justice – locked eyes with Jason, her gaze cold and unyielding.

"Jason, you're under arrest for harboring runaways," she announced, her voice tinged with disdain. "Rachel and Calisto were reported missing by their mothers earlier tonight."

"Wait, what?" Rachel stammered, her face a mix of shock and confusion. "We just came out to have some fun! We didn't runaway, we were just about to go back home!"

"Fun doesn't involve breaking the law," Officer Sue snapped back, ignoring the girls pleas, cuffing Jason's wrists behind his back. He struggled against her grip, desperate to break free and protect the girls from whatever punishment awaited them.

"Please, don't take them!" he pleaded, his voice raw with emotion. "They didn't do anything wrong! We were just playing laser tag!"

"Save it for the judge," Officer Sue retorted, shoving him toward the waiting police car. As he stumbled forward, he glanced back at Calisto and Rachel, their faces pale and tear-streaked. Consuelo stood nearby, trembling with fear. The weight of his actions, their unintended consequences, bore down on him like a crushing tidal wave. How could he have let this happen again? How could he have put the people he cared for most in danger?

"Take care of them!" Jason shouted over his shoulder as he was forced into the backseat of the police cruiser. "Promise me you'll take care of them!"

"Jason..." Calisto whispered, her voice barely audible above the roar of sirens and slamming car doors. But it was enough to pierce through the chaos, echoing in his mind as the vehicle pulled away. And as the distance between them grew, so too did the chasm within him, an abyss of regret and loss that threatened to consume him whole.

Jason sat on the hard mattress inside the steel bars of his jail cell, feeling an icy chill that had nothing to do with the temperature. On this Christmas Eve, instead of being surrounded by love and companionship, he was surrounded by despair and regret. He knew deep down that he had done his best to take care of the girls and the smaller boys in his group, protecting them from harm. But a phrase often echoed through his head—words that would later be spoken in a famous Hollywood movie: "Ever wonder if you are really just living a lie? What if you aren't actually the good guy pretending to be the bad guy. Maybe you are actually the bad guy pretending to be the good guy." Could he be pretending to be a villain? Or was he actually playing the role of a hero? He couldn't be sure, perhaps it was both. Could a person be both good and bad at once?

Startled back to reality by a gruff voice from across the cell, "Hey kid, you got any plans for today?" The older inmate, his face scarred by years of violence and addiction, chuckled darkly.

"Leave me alone," Jason muttered, his voice barely audible. He stared at the floor, doing his best to block out the other man's taunts. But they were only a cruel reminder of everything he'd lost.

"Suit yourself," the man replied with a sneer. He leaned back against the wall, lighting up a smuggled cigarette and filling the cell with acrid smoke.

Jason closed his eyes, trying to escape the nightmare that had become his reality. But every time he did, Calisto's face appeared before him – her beautiful, expressive eyes filled with tears as she watched him being taken away. That image haunted him, a constant reminder of how he had failed her and the others.

"Calisto…" he whispered, his voice choked with emotion. "I'm so sorry."

In the silence of the cell, his thoughts took on a life of their own – memories of happier times spent with his friends and family, laughing, talking, and enjoying each other's company. Those moments now seemed like distant dreams, torn away by the harsh consequences of his actions.

"Hey, you alright?" The older inmate's voice cut through Jason's reverie, his tone surprisingly gentle.

"Does it matter?" Jason snapped, his frustration boiling over. "I ruined everything. I destroyed my life, and I dragged them down with me."

"Listen, kid," the man said softly, the mocking tone gone from his voice. "I know what it's like to feel like you've got nothing left. But sometimes, the only way to make things right is to face the consequences and learn from them."

"Easy for you to say," Jason scoffed, anger giving way to despair once more. "You don't have to live with the knowledge that you hurt the people you care about most."

"Maybe not," the older inmate replied, taking a drag on his cigarette. "But I do know what it's like to lose everything and everyone you love. And let me tell you, kid – dwelling on the past won't change a damn thing."

As the man's words echoed in his mind, Jason couldn't help but consider their truth. He had made mistakes, terrible ones that had cost him dearly. But perhaps there was still hope, a chance to make amends and rebuild his life.

"Maybe you're right," he said quietly, looking up at the other man with newfound determination. "But first, I need to get out of here."

"Ha! Easier said than done, kid," the older inmate laughed, stubbing out his cigarette on the cold concrete floor. "But maybe, just maybe, you'll find a way."

For the first time since his arrest, Jason allowed himself a glimmer of hope – a tiny spark in the darkness that surrounded him. It wasn't much, but it was enough to fuel his resolve. He would find a way to make things right with

Calisto, Rachel, Consuelo, and the rest of his family – no matter what it took.

The cold steel bars of the jail cell cast long shadows across Jason's face as he sat on the edge of his bunk, lost in thought. Despite the clamor of the other inmates and the harsh overhead lights, the world beyond his confinement seemed to fade away. All that mattered was Calisto – her warm smile, the way her eyes sparkled when she laughed, and the comforting embrace that once made him feel invincible.

"Hey, kid," a gruff voice interrupted his reverie. Jason looked up to see Officer Sue standing at the entrance of his cell, her arms folded across her broad chest. Her rugged features were softened by a hint of concern, as if she could sense the turmoil raging within him.

"Got a minute?" she asked, her tone uncharacteristically gentle.

Rage filled Jason as he snapped back, "Get lost! I don't want anything to do with you!"

"Listen, I've seen a lot of kids like you come through here," Officer Sue began, shifting her weight from one foot to the other. "You're bright, talented, but caught up in a life that'll only lead to more trouble. I'm not going to sugarcoat it – if you don't make some changes, you're going to end up dead or in prison for a long, long time."

Jason swallowed hard, his throat suddenly dry. He knew she was right, but the weight of her words felt crushing. "So, what am I supposed to do?" he asked, his voice barely above a whisper.

"Ever heard of Job Corps?" Officer Sue inquired, raising an eyebrow. Jason shook his head, and she continued. "It's a government-run program that helps troubled youth get back on track. They provide job training, education, and housing." Officer Sue went on, "This isn't the way to live. Think about it - the people you're associating with aren't your true family. You have parents that will welcome you back home. These friends of yours won't stay loyal when it really matters; they'll drop you like a hot potato if it means saving their own skin. I know you care for the girls, but they too need an exit from this lifestyle and that may mean no longer being around you, however difficult that might be."

Jason listened to Officer Sue's words with a heavy heart. He wanted to believe that he could do better, that he could make a fresh start for himself and his family, but the reality of his situation kept crashing down on him like a wave. The possibility of leaving the gang lifestyle was daunting, but it was not impossible. He had seen others make it out alive, and if they could do it, so could he. But before he could move on, Jason had to find a way to mend things with Calisto, Rachel and Consuelo. Maybe it would be best if he walked away from everything for good and never looked back. He thought there was a possibility that his presence had caused the girls more trouble than good, so maybe it'd be better for them if he were gone.

Officer Sue reassured Jason that there was help available if he decided to take the Job Corps route – counselors would provide guidance and resources throughout the process, helping him find sustainable employment and housing close to home. It wasn't easy, she warned him – it would require hard work and dedication – but if he committed himself fully, there was no reason why he couldn't build a better life for himself. With that final piece of advice ringing in his ears, Jason thanked Officer Sue for her help and promised her that he would give serious consideration to what she said. As she left his cell, Jason felt an unfamiliar surge of optimism inside him; perhaps this could be his chance at redemption after all. He quickly stifled the thought before it could take root—if he failed again this time around, there might not be another opportunity. Only one thing was certain: if Jason wanted change in his life – real change – then he had to fight for it.

8

The Path To Success Starts Here

The courtroom was a graveyard of hushed whispers, every word swallowed by the imposing walls and high ceiling. Jason stood at the defendant's table, his tall, lanky frame dwarfed by the mahogany furniture and the weight of the trial. He could feel the stares boring into him - some of them curious, while others were hostile. The air was thick with anticipation as everyone awaited the judge's decision.

"Order in the court!" the bailiff barked, and the room snapped to attention. The judge, an older man with a stern expression and thinning gray hair, cleared his throat.

The judge addressed Jason, saying "You have been found guilty of a variety of charges concerning the harboring of minors. You have created an immense amount of trouble in this town and courtroom for some time now." his voice booming through the room like thunder. "However, given your age and lack of prior criminal record, and based on the recommendation from Officer Sue, I am inclined to give you a chance at rehabilitation."

He paused for effect, and Jason felt his heart pound against his ribcage, unsure of what was to come next. When the judge continued, it felt as if the whole world had stopped spinning for a moment.

"Instead of sentencing you to detention, I am ordering you to enroll in the Job Corps program. You will complete your education, receive vocational training, and develop life skills that will help you become a contributing member of society."

For a second, Jason couldn't believe what he was hearing. All his anger and resentment seemed to dissipate in an instant, replaced by a tiny glimmer of hope. But almost as quickly as it appeared, that hope was suffocated by doubt. Could someone like him really change? Was there anything left for him outside the gang life?

"Thank you, Your Honor," Jason managed to choke out, his voice cracking under the weight of emotions he didn't know how to express. He looked around the chamber, trying to spot a friendly face. His parents were in the audience - the only family he had left. Unfortunately, his friends and the girls weren't there.

"Young man, this is your opportunity to turn your life around," the judge said, his gaze fixed on Jason like a laser. "I strongly suggest you take it. You will complete an 18 month program, and if you fail, you will go to prison."

Jason left the courtroom with a flurry of ideas in his head. He saw it as an opportunity to start anew, but what if that didn't work out? Could he still go back to how things used to be? Get through this Job Corps program and back to the life he cherished? To the girl he loved so deeply?

The Job Corps office was a place of hope and promise, but also fear and apprehension. Jason had been told repeatedly that the program would change his life, but as he sat in the recruiter's office, taking in all the details, he couldn't shake the uneasiness. The center was located two hundred miles away, leaving him far from his family, friends and most importantly, Calisto. It seemed an eternity until graduation day would come, and all his current worries came flooding back to him. Would his newfound independence only lead to further trouble? Was it even possible for him to stay out of trouble with no one around to keep him in check? The recruiter seemed to sense the tension in the room; she leaned forward with her hands clasped together on her desk and smiled reassuringly at Jason. "Look," she said softly. "I understand your concerns, but this is a chance for you to start fresh. The Job Corps has helped many people just like you turn their lives around." Jason nodded slowly, feeling a bit more optimistic than before. He had nothing left here - only memories of what once was - so why not take a chance? He looked up at the recruiter with determination in his eyes and agreed to embark on this new journey. Days flew by in a blur as Jason made preparations for what lay ahead of him. On his last night in town he called Calisto for one final goodbye; it felt like letting go of an old part of himself that he could never get back again. It was these moments when he realized how much he truly cherished her and everything she had done for him over the months - all while trying desperately not to shed any tears as they talked for one last time. Finally, it was time to leave; with one last glance at his home town behind him, Jason boarded the bus heading towards his new life full of uncertainties yet promising

Jason stepped off the bus, a duffel bag slung over his shoulder. He tried not to think back to the life he left behind, but the memories clung to him like the cobwebs that adorned the old, dilapidated buildings.

"Welcome to Job Corps," a cheerful voice called out, pulling Jason's attention toward the facility ahead of him. It was a sprawling campus comprised of several brick buildings, surrounded by lush green lawns and towering trees. A sign stood proudly at the entrance, declaring its purpose: education, vocational training, and life skills for young people in need of a second chance.

"Hey there!" the voice said again, coming from a short, balding man with a clipboard in hand. "I'm Mr. Thompson, your counselor. You must be Jason."

"Uh, yeah." Jason nodded, shifting his weight uneasily.

"Great! Let me show you to your dorm." Mr. Thompson led the way, describing the various programs offered at Job Corps as they walked. "Now, we've got a mix of students here from all walks of life. Some are here to escape trouble, while others are simply looking for better opportunities."

Stepping through the doors of the dormitory, Jason noticed that there were separate floors for boys and girls. He was a bit intimidated to find out that this campus had previously been occupied by the criminally insane. "Well, at least I fit in," he laughed to himself.

As he was shown to his room, Jason hesitated at the threshold, taking in the small, cramped room. Three bunk beds lined the walls, each adorned with various personal items and photographs. It felt foreign, like stepping into another world.

"Let me introduce you to your dorm mates," Mr. Thompson said, gesturing to the other occupants. "That's Marcus, he's studying to be an electrician; There's Nathan, he's learning the landscaping trade; Luis over there is interested in culinary arts; and this is Aiden, our future computer repair guy."

Jason surveyed the faces before him, noting the tattoos and scars that hinted at deeper stories beneath the surface. This was not a group of friends, but a collection of strangers, each here to forge their own path.

"Hey," Jason muttered, offering a small, nervous smile. "I'm Jason."

In response to Jason, Marcus gave a curt nod and cast his eyes downward to the blue Dockers that Jason was wearing—the same style of clothing that his gang favored. As he noticed this, Jason felt a twinge of threat emanating from Marcus's appraisal.

"Welcome aboard," Luis said, extending a hand for Jason to shake. Aiden simply nodded, his attention focused on the book in front of him.

"Alright, I'll let you guys get settled," Mr. Thompson said, leaving the room with a final wave. "Remember, we're all here to help each other succeed."

As the door closed behind the counselor, an uneasy silence fell over the room. Jason could feel the weight of unspoken histories and rivalries bearing down on him, threatening to suffocate the fragile hope that had carried him this far. But as he looked around at his new dorm mates, he realized that they were all searching for the same thing: a chance at a better life.

"Hey, so… what brings you here?" Jason asked tentatively, breaking the silence.

"Needed a change, man," Marcus replied, leaning back against his bunk. "Gang life ain't all it's cracked up to be, you know?" Jason learned that Marcus was in a rival gang back home. "So much for escaping the life," Jason sighed to himself.

"Got kicked out of my last school," Luis admitted, shrugging nonchalantly. "Figured I'd give this a shot."

"Family issues," Aiden muttered, not looking up from his screen.

"Got in to too many fist fights back home, court ordered here," Nathan said sternly.

Jason nodded, understanding the weight behind each response. They were all running from something, hoping that Job Corps could provide the fresh start they so desperately needed. As he climbed onto his bunk, he couldn't help but wonder if it was possible for someone like him to truly change. But he knew he had to try – for himself, for Calisto, and for the girls he had left behind, still believing that he would return to them soon.

The shrill sound of the alarm pierced through Jason's dreams, yanking him back to reality. As he fumbled to silence the intrusive device, he squinted at the dimly lit room. The pale morning light filtered through the blinds, casting shadows across the faces of his dorm mates. An unfamiliar knot formed in his stomach as he remembered where he was – Job Corps.

"Man, I hate waking up this early," Marcus mumbled, rubbing his eyes and swinging his legs over the edge of the bunk.

"Same here," Luis agreed, stretching his arms above his head with a yawn.

Jason glanced at the clock on the wall, which read 6:00 AM. Back home, he'd still be fast asleep or out causing trouble with his gang. But this was his new life now, one that demanded discipline and punctuality. He swung his legs over the edge of his bunk, planting his feet firmly on the cold floor. Part of him wanted to dive back under the covers, to retreat into the familiar chaos of his past. But another part, one that had been buried deep within him for so long, whispered that change was possible – that he could break free from the chains of his old life.

"Alright," Jason said, steeling himself against the uncertainty that gnawed at the edges of his mind, "Let's get ready for class."

The days at Job Corps were tightly structured, each hour brimming with purpose and potential. After a quick breakfast, Jason and his dorm mates would split up, heading to their respective classes and vocational training sessions. For Jason, this meant grueling hours spent in front of a computer monitor, learning business management – a trade that he had chosen in an attempt to forge a new path for himself.

As he sat on the black rolling office chair, he couldn't help but feel like an imposter, a fraud masquerading as someone capable of change. The other students seemed to move with ease, their hands deftly maneuvering the keys on the keyboard. He looked down at his own fingers, wondering if he would ever feel as confident.

"Hey, man," Aiden said, sliding in beside him. "Need a hand?"

"Uh, yeah," Jason replied, grateful for the offer. "I can't seem to figure out where to start"

"Here, let me show you," Aiden offered, reaching for the mouse.

As they worked side by side, Jason couldn't help but marvel at the camaraderie that was beginning to form between them. It was a far cry from the brutal gang life he had known, where loyalty was forged in blood and betrayal lurked around every corner. But it also made him question whether he truly belonged here, amongst these hopeful souls striving for a better future.

"Great job today, guys," their instructor praised as the day's session came to an end. "Remember, practice makes perfect."

As they filed out of the workshop, Jason's thoughts drifted back to Calisto and the girls he had left behind. Would they be proud of him, or would they see him as a traitor, abandoning them for this new life? He clenched his fists tightly, vowing to prove not only to them but also to himself that he could make something of himself – that he could rise above the ashes of his past and forge a brighter path.

The morning sun cast long shadows across the courtyard as Jason and his fellow Job Corps students filed into the cafeteria. As he surveyed the bustling room, he couldn't help but feel a sense of awe at the variety of people who had been brought together by this program. To his left, he noticed a group of girls from various ethnicities laughing over breakfast, while on his right, an older man with graying hair discussed plans for the day's vocational training with a younger student.

"Hey, Jason!" called out Maria, a friendly girl with dark curls and a warm smile. "Come sit with us!"

91

He hesitated for a moment, then strode over to join Maria and her friends. As he took his seat, he found himself drawn into a conversation about the challenges they each faced in their respective programs.

"Man, I struggled so hard with those engine diagrams yesterday," Maria admitted. "But after today's class, I think I'll get the hang of it."

"Same here," chimed in another student, Derek, who sported a mohawk and multiple tattoos. "I never thought I'd enjoy learning about cooking, but it's actually pretty cool."

As the conversation flowed around him, Jason began to feel a growing sense of connection to his fellow students. Despite their diverse backgrounds and experiences, they were all united in their pursuit of a better life – a life free from gangs, violence, and poverty.

And it wasn't just the conversations that made him feel part of something bigger; it was also the hands-on learning experiences he had in the workshops. In his computer class, under the watchful eye of Mr. Thompson, Jason's nimble fingers worked deftly to type his way through his assignments. Jason had been using computers since an early age, so this was nothing new for him. In fact, he chose this particular vocational program in the hopes of finishing it quickly and getting back to his previous life.

"Great job, Jason," Mrs. Thompson said one afternoon, clapping him on the shoulder as she surveyed his handiwork. "Your progress is truly impressive."

"Thanks, Mrs. Thompson," Jason replied, a hint of pride creeping into his voice. "I never thought I'd be any good at this stuff, but I'm really starting to enjoy it."

As the weeks passed, Jason found himself growing more and more accustomed to the rhythm of life at Job Corps. He was learning practical skills that could help him build a successful career, and he was forming bonds with people who, like him, were seeking to break free from the chains of their past.

But even amidst this newfound sense of purpose, his thoughts would still often drift toward Calisto and the girls he had left behind. He knew that they were still grappling with the harsh realities of gang life, and he couldn't shake the feeling that he owed them some kind of debt – a debt that could only be repaid by using the opportunities provided by Job Corps to create a better life for himself and, in turn, for them.

"Hey, Jason!" Maria called out one day as they filed out of the workshop. "Wanna grab a bite to eat?"

"Sure," he replied, offering her a small smile. "Sounds good."

As they walked across campus together, Jason couldn't help but feel grateful for the chance he had been given. The road ahead was still long and fraught with uncertainty, but for the first time in his life, he felt as though he was truly moving forward – leaving the darkness of his past behind and stepping into the light of a brighter future.

The morning sun cast a warm glow through the windows of the Job Corps cafeteria, illuminating the faces of students from all walks of life as they chatted excitedly over breakfast. Jason sat among them, his eyes scanning the room while he absentmindedly picked at his scrambled eggs.

"Man, these rules are killing me," groaned Carlos, one of Jason's dorm mates and a fellow former gang member, as he slumped in his seat. "I can't even go out for a smoke without getting checked by security."

"Tell me about it," Jason muttered under his breath. The strict structure of Job Corps was indeed a challenge for him, but he knew that this discipline was essential to his transformation. He needed to shed the habits he had developed on the streets; after all, they had only led him to a darker path.

"Hey, have you heard about the new student?" Maria asked, her voice barely containing her enthusiasm. "Her name is Felicia and she'll be joining the Nursing program. I think you two would really get along, Jason." Jason perked up at the suggestion, intrigued by the idea of meeting someone new.

The news of Felicia's arrival had spread like wildfire throughout the Job Corps campus, and everyone was eager to meet her. When she finally arrived, everyone was struck by her beauty and intelligence – qualities that were reflected in her warm and kind demeanor. Soon enough, Jason and Felicia found themselves becoming fast friends. Despite their different backgrounds, they both shared a passion for learning and a desire to improve their lives through education. They talked for hours about their hopes for the future and how they planned to use the tools provided by Job Corps to reach their goals. Jason felt his heart swell with admiration as he listened to Felicia's stories of her childhood in along the coast; a childhood spent dodging gangs and struggling with poverty but which was ultimately filled with moments of joy and learning. He saw in her story an echo of his own experiences, albeit on opposite sides of the state. He found himself drawn to her optimism and strength in the face of adversity; it reminded him of Calisto's indomitable spirit back home. Word soon spread throughout campus that these two were becoming quite close, but neither minded as they continued to spend more time together talking, studying, or just enjoying each other's company in companionable silence. Their bond grew stronger every day as they encouraged one another on their respective paths towards success. Before long, Jason knew that this new found friendship had become something else entirely: love.

As Jason navigated his way through the challenges of Job Corps, he couldn't help but feel the weight of his past bearing down on him. The occasional whispers and stares from other students, rumors of his gang affiliations spreading like wildfire, made it difficult to fully embrace his new life.

"Yo, Jason," a burly student sneered one day in the game room, eyeing him with contempt. "I heard you used to run with some pretty bad dudes. What's the deal, huh? You think you're better than us now?"

"Look, man, I'm just trying to do my thing here and make something of myself," Jason replied defensively, his fists clenching as he fought to keep his anger in check. "I don't want any trouble."

"Whatever," the student scoffed, stalking away. But the encounter left Jason shaken, a reminder that the ghosts of his past would not be so easily banished.

Despite these setbacks, however, Jason continued to thrive in his chosen vocational pursuit. Under the watchful eye of Mr. Johnson, he quickly became adept at the many different software programs the students were learning in the business class. In fact, Jason had become so skilled, the instructor, Mrs. Thompson challenged him to a typing contest, which Jason won handedly, surprising the teacher and the students alike.

"Jason, you've got a real talent for this," Mr. Johnson remarked one afternoon as he inspected the latest progress report. "Keep up the good work, and I can see you going far in this field."

"Thanks, Mr. Johnson," Jason mumbled, feeling both humbled and encouraged by his counselor's praise. As he wiped the nervous sweat from his hands, he couldn't help but wonder if, through his determination and hard work, he might finally break free of the shadows that haunted him – not only for his own sake but also for the loved ones he had left behind.

The sun dipped below the horizon, splashing warm hues of red and orange across the sky as Jason stood on the outskirts of the Job Corps campus. He took a deep breath, filling his lungs with the crisp winter air, and tried to make sense of the whirlwind of emotions that swirled within him.

"Hey, Jason!" called out a friendly voice. It was Marcus, one of the few students he had grown close to during his time at Job Corps. "We're gonna catch a movie in the rec room, wanna join?"

"Sure," Jason replied, grateful for the distraction. As they walked towards the recreation center, Jason found himself reflecting on the past few months. Despite the challenges he had faced – the strict rules, difficult classmates, and personal obstacles – he couldn't deny the positive impact Job Corps had made on his life. He had discovered a passion and talent for computers, gained valuable skills, and forged new friendships that transcended the boundaries of his gang-affiliated past.

"Man, I can't believe how far you've come since you got here," Marcus remarked, evidently picking up on Jason's introspective mood. "I remember when you first arrived, looking all lost and unsure of yourself."

Jason chuckled, realizing how true Marcus's words were. "Yeah, I didn't know what to expect when I got here. But this place has given me a chance to start over, you know? A shot at a better future."

"Definitely," Marcus agreed, nodding. "It's not always easy, but it's worth it."

As they settled into their seats in the rec room, surrounded by fellow students laughing and chatting, Jason felt a surge of gratitude towards the Job Corps program. This place had provided him with a safe haven, an opportunity to escape the dangerous grip of gang life and forge a new path for himself. The structured environment, though initially jarring, had instilled in him a sense of discipline and purpose he had never known before.

"Hey," Jason said quietly, turning to Marcus as the movie began to play. "I just wanted to say thanks for being there for me. I know I haven't always been the easiest person to get along with, but your support has meant a lot."

"Of course, man," Marcus replied, clapping him on the back. "We're all in this together, right? Besides, I can see the change in you – you're more focused, more determined than ever. That's something to be proud of."

Jason nodded, his gaze fixed on the flickering images on the screen, but his thoughts far away. He knew that he still had a long road ahead of him, that the specter of his past would continue to haunt him even as he worked tirelessly to build a better life. But now, for the first time in as long as he could remember, he felt hope – hope that one day, he might truly overcome the darkness that had once consumed him and step into a brighter future. And for that, he was grateful beyond measure.

As the sun dipped below the horizon, casting the Job Corps campus in a warm orange glow, Jason stood alone on the edge of the basketball court. The sound of laughter and conversation filled the air as his fellow students enjoyed their free time, but for once, he wasn't drawn to join them. Instead, he stared into the distance, his thoughts consumed by the life he had left behind.

"Yo, J!" called out one of his new friends, Terry, from across the court. "You gonna come play or what?"

"Maybe later," Jason replied, forcing a smile onto his face before returning to his contemplation.

He couldn't help but worry about the girls he had left back home, the young women he had sworn to protect as part of his gang. Had they managed to find safety without him? Were they even alive? And then there was Calisto – beautiful, captivating Calisto, who had become his entire world before it all came crashing down. The thought of her being swept up in the chaos and violence he had escaped made his heart ache with a mixture of longing and guilt.

"Man, you've been standing here forever," Marcus said, appearing beside him with a concerned expression. "What's eating you?"

Jason hesitated, debating whether to share his inner turmoil with his friend. But something about Marcus' steady gaze convinced him that it was safe to open up.

"Calisto," he admitted, the name tasting bittersweet on his tongue. "I can't stop thinking about her. And the girls I left behind... I just hope they're okay."

"Look," Marcus said gently, placing a hand on Jason's shoulder. "I know it's hard, but you can't change the past. All you can do is focus on the future – your future. You've got so much potential, man. Don't waste it worrying about things you can't control."

Jason nodded, realizing the truth in Marcus' words. He had been given a chance at a fresh start, an opportunity to build a new life away from the darkness that had once threatened to swallow him whole. But as much as he wanted to embrace that future with open arms, it was impossible to forget the people he had left behind.

"Promise me something," he said, turning to face his friend. "Promise me that no matter what happens, we'll always have each other's backs – here and beyond Job Corps."

"Of course," Marcus replied without hesitation, his eyes shining with sincerity. "You've got my word."

With that vow hanging in the air between them, Jason felt a newfound resolve settle within him. The road ahead would undoubtedly be fraught with challenges and obstacles, but he was determined to navigate it with courage and determination. He would continue to grow and transform at Job Corps, building a foundation for a brighter future – not just for himself, but for those he still cared deeply about.

"Alright," he said finally, his voice filled with quiet conviction. "Let's go play some ball."

9

A New Love Blossoms

The winter snowflakes fell gently, blanketing the ground in a soft white layer that muffled the sound of footsteps. The fresh cold air filled Jason's lungs as he walked hand in hand with Felicia, feeling invigorated by the mere touch of her warm hands. Her emerald eyes shone brightly, reflecting the joy that radiated from her every being. She was a beautiful nursing student, with short auburn hair cascading down her neck like a waterfall.

"Isn't it just lovely?" she asked, her breath visible in the icy air as they strolled through the scenic landscape of the Job Corps campus. "I've always loved winter. There's something so peaceful about it."

Jason nodded and smiled, his blue eyes crinkling at the corners. "Yeah, it's beautiful," he agreed, but his heart was heavy. He couldn't help but feel guilty about how he left Calisto behind. The memory of her beauty haunted him, a constant reminder of the life he had abandoned for this newfound love.

As they walked, Felicia squeezed his hand tighter, sensing his inner turmoil. "You're awfully quiet today, Jason. What's on your mind?"

He hesitated, his gaze fixed on the snow-covered ground. The weight of his past threatened to crush him, and he knew he needed to open up to Felicia if their relationship was going to flourish. "I'm just thinking about Calisto," he confessed, his voice barely audible above the gentle crunching of their steps in the snow.

"Your ex-girlfriend?" Felicia asked softly, her eyes searching his face for any sign of lingering attachment.

"Kind of," Jason replied, his voice tinged with regret. "She was more than that, though. She was… She was my family, you know? Back when I was still part of the gang, she and the others were all I had. And now that I'm here, trying to build a new life with you… it's hard not to feel guilty about leaving her behind."

Felicia stopped walking and pulled Jason into an embrace, her arms wrapping around him tightly. "It's okay to feel guilty, Jason," she whispered, her breath warm against his ear. "But remember, you're here because you made a choice - a choice to change your life for the better and escape the cycle of violence you were trapped in. You can't blame yourself for wanting more than that life could ever offer."

Jason closed his eyes, allowing Felicia's words to seep into his very soul. He knew she was right, but the guilt still gnawed at him. As they stood there in the cold winter air, he realized that the love blossoming between them was as fragile as the snowflakes that continued to fall around them. But it was also just as beautiful, and he silently vowed to nurture and protect it, even as he mourned the loss of what he had left behind.

"Jason, I know Calisto meant a lot to you," Felicia said, her hand warm and comforting in his own. "But it's important for you to fully embrace this new chapter of your life. Dwelling on the past won't bring you happiness or peace."

"I know," he replied, his voice tinged with regret. "It's just hard to let go. She was my first love, and our lives were so deeply intertwined back then."

"Life is full of choices, Jason," Felicia said, gently squeezing his hand. "The choices we make define us, but they don't have to trap us. You've already taken the hardest step by leaving that world behind."

The duo strolled beneath the leaf-covered branches, now blanketed with snow, their branches sparkling in the winter sunlight. Jason finally allowed himself to believe her words. He could feel the shackles of his past loosening, replaced with an overwhelming desire to protect and cherish the love he shared with Felicia.

"Hey," she said, nudging him playfully. "You seem lost in thought. What are you thinking about?"

"New beginnings," Jason told her, a small smile playing at the corners of his lips. "And how grateful I am to have you by my side."

"Me too," Felicia whispered, leaning in for a tender kiss. Their lips met, and in that moment, Jason knew that he had found something worth fighting for – a love that would help him leave his old life in the rearview mirror.

"Thank you," he said, his voice barely above a whisper as they paused beneath a towering oak tree, its branches swaying gently in the breeze.

"For what?" Felicia asked, her eyes filled with warmth and affection.

"For helping me see that I can be more than my past," Jason replied, his heart swelling with gratitude. "For showing me that it's never too late to change."

"Change comes from within, Jason," she told him, a knowing smile on her face. "I just helped you find the strength you already had inside."

When spring came around, Jason was filled with a fresh burst of enthusiasm for his new life. With Felicia by his side, he threw himself into his studies. He contemplated how he could make a difference in the world when he graduated from Job Corps; how he could use his experience to help other young people stay away from the same temptations and problems that almost got him. He was dead set on making an impact and helping others avoid the same mistakes as him.

As he walked hand-in-hand with Felicia one warm evening, their laughter mingling with the gentle hum of cicadas, Jason couldn't help but marvel at how far he'd come. The gangster life that had once defined him now felt like a distant memory, replaced by a newfound sense of purpose, love, and hope for the future.

A chill ran down Jason's spine as he read the words on the crumpled piece of paper in his hands. Nate, one of his old gang friends, had attempted to rob a taco drive-through and was shot and killed by police during his getaway. The news shook him to his core. As if that wasn't enough, Ryan, barely eighteen years old, had been arrested for manufacturing and selling Meth. Felicia, sensing his distress, wrapped her arms around him, offering silent comfort.

"Are you okay?" she asked, concern lacing her voice.

"Two of my old friends …" he trailed off, unable to meet her gaze. "Nate…he was shot by the police during a robbery, they killed him."

Felicia's eyes widened in horror as she listened to the tragic news. "I'm so sorry," she whispered, her arms tightening around him.

"I can't help but feel guilty," Jason confessed, his voice cracking under the weight of his emotions. "If I were still back in town instead of here at Job Corps, I might've been driving the getaway car. Maybe things would have turned out differently."

"Hey," Felicia said gently, lifting his chin so their eyes met. "You can't blame yourself for his choices. You made the decision to change your life, and that's something to be proud of."

As they stood there in the fading light, Jason couldn't shake the feeling that he had abandoned his friends. He thought about Nate's infectious laugh and how they used to stay up all night talking about their dreams, never imagining that one day they'd be living a nightmare. And Ryan, scrawny and short but full of energy, always ready for a fight. His loyalty knew no bounds.

"Ryan…he got arrested," Jason choked out, his throat tight with emotion. "For cooking and selling Meth."

"Jason, listen to me," Felicia said firmly, her eyes filled with determination. "You can't go back and change the past. You have a chance to make something of yourself now, and you owe it to yourself to take it. You need to think about where you would be right now if you were back there. Maybe it would be you that would have been arrested, or even worse, shot dead by the police. You are here because you made the decision to better yourself and to pull yourself out of that life."

He knew she was right. Dwelling on what could have been wouldn't bring them back or save them from their own choices. He had escaped that life, and as much as it pained him to admit it, he couldn't save everyone.

"Promise me you'll stay focused on your future," Felicia implored, her eyes pleading for his commitment.

"I promise," Jason whispered, the weight of his past still heavy on his shoulders. But deep down, he understood that by striving towards a better future, he could be a beacon of hope for others who found themselves trapped in the same dark world he'd left behind.

And with that promise, Jason slowly began to let go of the guilt that had haunted him since leaving his old life behind. He would face each day with renewed determination, knowing that while he couldn't change the past, he could still make a difference in the future.

Jason sat on a bench, his fingers drumming nervously on his knees. His thoughts swirled around Rachel, Consuelo, and Calisto, as well as little Jessie and Johnnie. He wished he could reach out to them, offer some kind of guidance or support. They had to be so scared, living back in the neighborhood where everything is crumbling down around them. But he knew that part of his life was over; he couldn't go back. He could only hope that maybe one day they too would be given the chance to escape the situations they face.

"Hey," Felicia's soft voice broke through his thoughts as she approached, concern etched across her face. "You've been sitting out here for a while. Are you okay?"

"Kinda," Jason admitted, his blue eyes meeting hers. "I can't help but worry about everyone back home, especially the younger ones."

Felicia sat down beside him, her hand gently squeezing his. "I understand, Jason. But you can't save them all. You have to focus on your own future now."

"I know," he sighed, his eyes drifting towards the setting sun. "It's just hard, you know? I wish there was something I could do."

"Sometimes the best thing you can do is lead by example," Felicia offered, her dark eyes full of sincerity. "Show them that there's a way out, that they don't have to stay trapped in that life."

"Maybe," Jason conceded, hope flickering within him. "But it feels like I'm abandoning them."

"Jason," Felicia said firmly, gripping his hand tighter, "you're not abandoning them. You're breaking the cycle, and that's incredibly brave."

He smiled weakly at her, grateful for her unwavering support. They sat in silence for a moment, the last rays of sunlight fading from the sky.

"Let's talk about something else," Felicia suggested, trying to lift his spirits. "What do you want to do after Job Corps? Where do you see yourself in a few years?"

"Actually, I've been thinking about that," Jason said, his eyes brightening with excitement. "I want to become a social worker. Maybe I can help other kids avoid the mistakes I made."

Felicia's face lit up at his words. "That's an amazing idea, Jason. You'd be perfect for that."

"Thanks," he replied, his heart swelling with pride. "What about you? What do you want to do?"

"I'm going to finish nursing school and maybe specialize in pediatrics. I love working with kids," she shared, her passion evident.

"Sounds like a plan," Jason grinned, giving her hand a gentle squeeze as they began discussing their future together.

As the days turned into weeks, Felicia and Jason grew even closer, finding solace and strength in each other's company. They spent time together between classes, studying side by side in the library or sharing lunch in the cafeteria. And each night before curfew, they would take long walks around the campus, talking about their dreams and aspirations.

As spring approached, new life bloomed all around them, and Jason felt himself starting to truly heal from his past. With Felicia by his side, he was determined to build a better future – not just for himself, but as a guiding light for those he had left behind.

One evening, as rain pattered against the rec room windows, Jason and Felicia settled onto a worn couch to watch a movie. The flickering light from the screen cast shadows across their faces, emphasizing the intensity in Jason's blue eyes.

"Hey, I heard this one is pretty good," Felicia said, reading the DVD case for "Where The Day Takes You." "It's about a teen boy who takes care of his group of friends, like a makeshift family."

"Sounds interesting," Jason replied absently, his thoughts heavy with worry for his old gang. He hoped that they would find their way, just like he was trying to.

As the movie unfolded, Jason found himself drawn into the story, seeing reflections of his own life in the main character's struggles. His heart clenched painfully as the protagonist fought to protect his friends, even as it led him down a dangerous path.

"Jason, are you okay?" Felicia asked, noticing the tears streaming down his face.

"Sorry, I just…" Jason choked out, unable to find the words. "This movie… it feels like it's telling my story."

Felicia wrapped her arm around him, pulling him close. "Tell me about it, Jason. Tell me about where you came from before Job Corps. I know some of the details, but please, open up and tell me everything."

In a trembling voice, Jason began to share stories he had never told anyone – tales of loyalty and love, betrayal and loss. He spoke of the family he had created among his friends, and how it had all fallen apart. As he talked, he could feel the weight of his past lifting slightly, buoyed by Felicia's understanding and compassion.

"Thank you for sharing that with me, Jason," she whispered when he finished, pressing a soft kiss to his cheek. "You've come so far since then, and I know you'll continue to grow even stronger."

"Only because I have you by my side," he murmured, his heart aching with gratitude. "I don't know what I'd do without you."

"Let's always be there for each other, okay?" Felicia promised, her eyes shining with love.

"Deal," Jason agreed, sealing their pact with a tender kiss.

In the days that followed, Jason and Felicia grew ever closer, their bond forged by shared dreams and unspoken understanding. They were inseparable, a beacon of hope and love in a world often filled with darkness. These two young souls, forever changed by the power of love and the courage to face their pasts.

10

A Life Derailed By Deception

The scent of freshly cut grass filled the air as Jason and Felicia strolled through the job corps campus, hand in hand. The sun shone brightly overhead, casting a warm glow on the newly bloomed flowers that lined the walkways. It was the beginning of summer, and their laughter rang through the grounds like a sweet melody.

"Jason, I'm so proud of you," Felicia said, her brown eyes sparkling with admiration. "You've come such a long way since you first got here."

"Thanks, Felicia," he replied, giving her hand a gentle squeeze. He gazed into her eyes, feeling grateful for her unwavering support. "I couldn't have done it without you."

As they continued to walk, Jason couldn't help but feel a sense of accomplishment swelling within him. He had graduated from the Job Corp's business management program earlier in June, becoming one of the fastest graduates in campus history. To top it off, he had been offered a two-year free college scholarship – an opportunity that felt almost too good to be true. He'd be able to live at the Job Corp campus while attending school, and they would pick up all expense.

"Can you believe it, Felicia?" he mused aloud, his blue eyes reflecting the sky above. "A few months ago, I never would have thought I'd be standing here, holding your hand, and preparing for college. Life is full of surprises, huh?"

Felicia smiled warmly, her gaze never leaving his face. "It sure is, Jason. But you deserve every bit of success that comes your way. You've worked hard for this."

He let out a deep breath, his chest filling with pride. "I can't wait to see where this journey takes me. With you by my side, I feel like anything is possible."

As they paused beneath the shade of a towering oak tree, Jason wrapped his arm around Felicia's waist, drawing her closer. They stood there for a moment, simply taking in the beauty of the campus and the promise of their future together.

"Hey, you know what?" Jason said suddenly, a grin spreading across his face. "Let's make a pact right here, right now. No matter where life takes us, we'll always stick together. Deal?"

Felicia nodded, her eyes shining with determination. "Deal."

With that, they sealed their pact with a tender kiss beneath the oak tree – a symbol of strength and endurance in the face of life's unpredictable twists and turns. In this moment, Jason felt on top of the world, knowing that with Felicia by his side, he was ready to embrace whatever challenges lay ahead, confident in the knowledge that brighter days were on the horizon.

The summer sun cast a warm glow on the job corps campus as Jason and Felicia strolled hand in hand, their laughter echoing through the air. With his recent graduation from the business management program and a two-year college scholarship secured, Jason couldn't help but feel optimistic about their future. They had grown close over the past few months, and he knew that what they shared was special.

But as they wandered the lush, green grounds, an envious gaze observed them from a distance. Shelly, a girl who had harbored feelings for Jason since they first crossed paths at job corps, clenched her fists in frustration as she watched the happy couple.

Her heart raced with jealousy, her mind clouded by thoughts of what might have been if it were her walking beside him instead of Felicia. She couldn't stand to see them together any longer – something had to be done, she thought, to separate them and give her a chance to claim Jason's affections.

"Hey, Shelly!" a passing friend called out, but she barely acknowledged the greeting, her eyes never leaving Jason and Felicia. Her chest tightened with a bitter resentment as she watched them embrace beneath the shade of an oak tree.

"Jason should be mine," she muttered under her breath, her nails digging into her palms. "I can't let her take him away from me."

Shelly made her way to the campus security office, her resolve hardening with each step. She knew that drastic measures had to be taken if she wanted to eliminate the bond between Jason and Felicia.

"Excuse me," she said, her voice trembling as she approached the security officer on duty. "I need to report something… I don't know who else to turn to."

"Of course," the officer replied, concern etched across his face. "What seems to be the problem?"

Shelly paused, taking a deep breath to steady her nerves. "It's about Jason," she began, her voice wavering. "I saw him outside of campus… and he pulled a gun on me."

The security officer's eyes widened as he listened to Shelly embellish the fabricated tale, her fear and concern for her safety seeming all too genuine. He assured her that they would take the matter seriously and do everything in their power to investigate.

As Shelly left the security office, she couldn't help but feel a twisted sense of satisfaction. She knew that if Jason were removed from the job corps campus, it might give her the opportunity she so desperately craved – a chance to win his heart without Felicia in the picture, not taking into effect the full measure of what she had just done.

In her mind, she justified her actions as necessary for love. But in truth, she had set in motion a chain of events that would shatter not only Jason's dreams but also the trust and support he had built with those around him. And as the sun dipped below the horizon, casting shadows across the now-empty campus, the consequences of her actions loomed large, ready to change the course of their lives forever.

The sun's dying rays glinted off the metal locker, casting a warm glow over Jason's small room in the job corps dormitory. He had just finished packing his textbooks and was looking forward to grabbing dinner with Felicia before they tackled their assignments together. The air hummed with anticipation as he zipped up his backpack, unaware that his life was about to change forever.

A sudden knock on the door startled him, and before he could call out, the door swung open to reveal two stern-faced security officers. Their eyes immediately locked onto his tall, lanky frame, scrutinizing every detail as if searching for a hidden threat.

"Jason?" one of them asked, his voice cold and authoritative.

"Y-yeah, that's me," Jason stammered, taken aback by the intrusion. "What's going on?"

"Routine search," the other officer replied, stepping into the room without waiting for an invitation. The first officer followed suit, and both men began combing through his belongings with practiced efficiency.

Jason's heart raced, a mixture of confusion and fear bubbling up inside him. What were they looking for? Had he done something wrong? His thoughts raced back to the pellet gun he kept in his locker for security purposes, a precautionary measure against potential threats. But it wasn't a real firearm – surely that wouldn't be an issue, would it?

"Hey, what's this?" the second officer called out, holding up the pellet gun with a frown. Jason's stomach dropped like a stone.

"Uh, that's just a pellet gun," he stammered. "It's not a real gun or anything."

The first officer fixed him with an icy stare. "You know we have a zero tolerance policy when it comes to weapons on campus, right?"

"Of course, but I didn't think—"

"Didn't think?" the officer cut him off, his voice rising. "This is serious, Jason. You could be expelled for this."

"Expelled?" Jason's voice cracked, disbelief and panic coursing through him. "No, please, I didn't mean any harm. It's just for protection."

"Regardless of your intentions," the second officer interjected, "rules are rules. We can't make exceptions."

Jason's mind raced with thoughts of Felicia, their plans for the future, the scholarship he'd worked so hard to earn. All of it seemed to disintegrate before his eyes as the security officers continued their search. Images of his parents' disappointment and confusion flashed through his mind, adding to the growing weight in his chest.

"Please," he begged, desperation lacing his voice. "I'll get rid of it. Just give me a chance to prove that I'm not a threat."

The first officer shook his head, his expression unyielding. "I'm sorry, Jason. You'll have to come with us."

As they led him out of the room, Jason felt the familiar tendrils of panic and despair clawing at the edges of his consciousness, threatening to drag him back into the darkness he'd fought so hard to escape. But this time, it wasn't just his own future at stake – it was the relationships he'd forged, the love he'd found, and the life he'd built on the cusp of true success.

"Please," he whispered again, knowing that the plea would fall on deaf ears. "Don't do this."

"Hands behind your back," the first officer ordered, snapping cuffs around Jason's wrists. The cold metal bit into his skin, a chilling reminder of the reality he now faced.

"Wait," Jason said, his voice cracking as panic surged through him. "I need to tell Felicia. I can't just leave like this."

The second officer gripped his arm, forcing him to start walking. "There's no time for that. You're being removed from campus immediately."

The urgency in the officer's tone left no room for negotiation. As they escorted him through the halls, Jason's heart pounded painfully against his ribcage. Each step away from his room felt like an irreversible loss, a tearing away from the life he had built here. He glanced around, desperately searching for any familiar face, any chance to say goodbye.

But the hallways were empty, as if the universe was conspiring to isolate him from the people he cared about most.

"Please," Jason choked out, struggling to keep his composure. "Just let me see her. I can't disappear without saying something."

"Sorry, kid," the first officer replied, his voice devoid of sympathy. "You should have thought about the consequences before you broke the rules."

As they pushed him out onto the campus grounds, the late afternoon sun cast long shadows across the paths and buildings. The air was heavy with the scent of freshly cut grass, a cruel reminder of the summer days he had spent with Felicia, laughing and dreaming of their future together. Now, it seemed those dreams were slipping through his fingers like sand.

Unable to contain his anguish any longer, Jason's vision blurred with tears. How could one mistake unravel everything he had worked so hard for? His stomach churned with a mixture of guilt and anger – at himself for letting his loved ones down, at Shelly for her jealousy-fueled sabotage, at the unforgiving system that had deemed him disposable.

"Please," he whispered once more, the word barely audible through his ragged breaths. "I don't want to lose everything."

But even as he pleaded, he knew it was too late. The officers' grip on his arms was unyielding, and the campus gates loomed large in front of them. As they dragged him away from the life he'd known, Jason's heart ached with the bitter sting of loss and the overwhelming weight of an uncertain future. Within minutes, Jason had been brought a duffel bag with his clothing, and escorted to the local bus depot, where he was put on a bus headed across the state, back to the home he had all but forgotten.

His Dad was waiting for him when the bus arrived. Jason was taken back to his dad's house. The house he had grown up in, the house he had once lived in as a child. All the memories of childhood came flooding back to him as they pulled into the driveway. The front door creaked open, casting a sliver of light across the darkened hallway. Jason stepped into the house, his shoulders slumped under the weight of his duffel bag and the crushing disappointment that accompanied him home. The silence was deafening, swallowing every echo of the laughter he had left behind at the job corps campus. Gone were the sounds of students chatting beneath trees or rushing to classes; in their place was the quiet emptiness that seemed to seep into every corner of his life.

The atmosphere in the room was thick with tension. His father stood silently, arms crossed as he stared Jason down. His mom, who had been living separately from his dad for years, had arrived to join the conversation, her own disappointment weighing heavy on her expression. Jason felt like he could barely breathe as his parents began to speak. His dad went first, his words laced with disappointment and anger as he listed off all the mistakes Jason had made and the consequences that would come with them. His mom followed suit soon after. Her voice was softer than his fathers but carried a pained sadness as she reeled off all of the alternative routes Jason should have taken. As they spoke, Jason's guilt and sorrow deepened. He hung his head in shame, unable to meet their eyes despite knowing how important it was for him to do so. When they finished listing off his indiscretions and potential sentences that could follow, all three of them lapsed into silence once more. For a long time they sat there in silence until finally, his mom spoke up again: "Jason [she said], I know you heard us, I know you understand what you did wrong - so what are you going to do about it?" That one simple question seemed to cut through all of the noise in Jason's head. He looked up at her then finally nodded; it was time he took responsibility for himself and stopped letting others control him. Taking a deep breath, he began telling them about his plan: go back to court and plead for mercy since he didn't complete 18 months in the program, look into job opportunities within the community that might help build some experience while also being able to provide financially — anything to keep himself out of trouble. His parents listened quietly as he outlined his plan before eventually both nodding in agreement.

"Thanks, Mom. Thanks, Dad," Jason whispered, overcome with gratitude for his parents' unwavering support. But even as the words left his lips, he couldn't shake the feeling that he had somehow failed them – and himself – in ways that could never be repaired.

The sun dipped below the horizon, casting its final orange glow across Jason's bedroom. He stood at the window, clenching his fists in frustration as he watched neighborhood kids laughing and playing on the street. They seemed so carefree, while his world had come crashing down around him.

"Damn it," he muttered under his breath, slamming his fist against the windowsill. The sting of pain did little to quell the anger bubbling beneath the surface. He couldn't help but feel defeated by circumstances beyond his control – Shelly and her lies, the campus security's hasty actions, and now, the loss of everything he had worked for. It all felt so unfair and it felt very familiar, like life was repeating itself.

As he struggled to make sense of it all, Jason's phone buzzed on his bed. Snatching it up, he saw Felicia's number flash across the screen. His heart leapt at the sight, and for a moment, he hesitated. He knew this conversation would be painful, but he couldn't avoid it forever.

"Hey," he said quietly, his voice cracking as he answered the call.

"Jason… I can't believe what happened," Felicia whispered, her voice trembling with emotion. "I never thought… I mean, how could they just kick you out like that?"

"Because they don't care about the truth," Jason spat bitterly, his anger momentarily flaring. "All they see is some gangbanger with a gun, and suddenly, I'm a threat."

"Jason, you're not a threat," Felicia insisted, her voice firm. "You're one of the kindest, smartest people I know. You've got a big heart, and I know you didn't mean for any of this to happen."

He sighed, his eyes welling with tears as he stared at the fading sunlight outside. "Doesn't matter now," he said, swallowing hard. "I'm back home, and there's nothing I can do about it."

"Hey," Felicia said softly, determination in her voice. "You're not giving up, are you? You've come so far, Jason. Don't let this one setback ruin your chances at a better future."

"Thanks, Felicia," he whispered, touched by her unwavering faith in him. "I don't know what I'd do without you."

"Promise me something," she said, her voice cracking. "Promise me you won't give up on yourself... no matter how hard things get."

"I promise," he replied, his voice thick with emotion. "As long as you promise to keep in touch, okay?"

"Of course," she agreed, sniffing back tears. "We'll talk soon, I promise."

"Goodbye, Felicia," he whispered, his heart heavy as they exchanged their final words.

"Goodbye, Jason." And with that, the line went dead, leaving him to face the quiet emptiness of his room – and the uncertainty of his future – alone. It was clear to them both that this could very well be their final conversation, and it turned out to be exactly that.

The silence hung heavily in the air as Jason stared at the now lifeless phone, the weight of his situation settling in. His bedroom felt suffocating and foreign - a stark contrast to the bustling job corps campus he had called home for months.

"Damn it," he muttered under his breath, his frustration mounting. He paced back and forth, the worn floorboards creaking beneath him. The room seemed to shrink with each step, trapping him just like the circumstances that had led to his expulsion.

"Jason?" His mother's voice filtered through the thin wall, muffled and concerned. "Are you okay in there?"

"Yeah, Mom," he replied, forcing a steadiness into his voice he didn't feel. "Just… sorting things out."

"Alright," she conceded, her tone hesitant. "Your father and I are here if you need us."

"Thanks," he said, grateful for their support but knowing they couldn't truly understand the depth of his emotions.

With a deep breath, Jason forced himself to sit on the edge of his bed, his hands gripping the worn sheets tightly. He glanced around at the faded posters adorning the walls, memories of a time before the promise of a brighter future had beckoned him away from home. Now, he was back where he started, all because of a jealous girl's lies and a zero tolerance policy that refused to listen to reason.

"Damn you, Shelly," Jason whispered, his eyes narrowing as he thought of the girl who had cost him everything. His heart ached for Felicia, for the friends he'd left behind without a chance to say goodbye, and for the dreams that now seemed so far out of reach.

"Maybe I should've known better," he mused aloud, self-doubt creeping in. "I shouldn't have kept that stupid pellet gun. But how am I supposed to trust anyone after what happened?"

He shook his head, trying to push the thoughts away, but they refused to budge. As he stared at the ceiling, memories of summer nights spent with Felicia on the job corps campus filled his mind, taunting him with what he had lost.

"Maybe Felicia's right," he thought, remembering her words of encouragement. "Maybe I can still make something of myself, even after this setback."

But as the shadows grew longer and night settled in, Jason couldn't escape the crushing loneliness that enveloped him like a shroud. He knew that no matter how hard he tried, he would never be able to fully trust the world again - not after seeing firsthand how easily it could turn against him.

"Promise me you won't give up on yourself... no matter how hard things get." Felicia's words echoed in his ears, both a comfort and a challenge.

"Alright, Felicia," he whispered into the darkness, determination flickering like a weak flame within him. "I won't give up. But I need to find my own way now."

With that, Jason lay down on his bed, his eyes fixed on the ceiling as the silence of the house pressed in around him. The future loomed ahead, uncertain and terrifying, and there was only one thing he knew for sure: nothing would ever be the same again.

11

Rising From The Ashes

The heavy wooden doors of the courtroom creaked open as Jason entered, his heart pounding in his chest. The same judge who had sentenced him to 18 months at Job Corps now held his fate once again. Sweat trickled down the back of his neck, and he struggled to swallow past the lump that had formed in his throat. He had been kicked out of Job Corps after just 8 months, and now he could be facing a lengthy jail sentence if the judge decided to come down hard on him.

"Jason Himes," the judge called out, peering over her half-moon glasses. Jason's legs felt like jelly as he made his way to the front of the courtroom. He tried to keep his face neutral, but he couldn't help the way his hands shook by his sides.

"Your Honor," the prosecutor began, riffling through a stack of papers, "The defendant was given an opportunity to turn his life around at Job Corps, and yet he threw it all away before even completing half of his term. It's clear that he hasn't taken this chance seriously, and we believe further punishment is necessary."

"Young man," the judge addressed Jason directly, "do you have anything to say for yourself?"

"Your Honor," Jason stammered, wiping his sweaty palms on his pants, "I know I messed up at Job Corps, but I did try my best. I got good grades in my classes and even learned some new skills." His voice wavered as he continued, "It wasn't easy being away from home, and I struggled to fit in. But I want to do better. I don't want to end up in jail."

"According to your records," the judge said, flipping through the pages in front of her, "you did indeed make some progress while at Job Corps. However, your dismissal due to breaking the rules is troubling. "

Jason's heart sank as he remembered the incident that had led to his expulsion. "Your Honor, I had the pellet gun in my locker as a safety precaution, that's all. It can be a dangerous place for a former gang member to be and I didn't want anyone messing with me."

"Yes but, " the prosecutor interjected, "while we understand that you may have felt threatened in that situation, it's important to remember that there are other ways to handle conflicts without the need to break the rules."

Jason nodded, knowing the prosecutor was right. However, Jason, feeling insecure without his supportive friends there to protect him, believed he had done what was right at the time.

"Your Honor," Jason pleaded, "I know I've made mistakes, but I don't want my whole life to be defined by them. I want a chance to prove that I can do better and make something of myself. Do bear in mind that I did indeed complete my vocational program, and I managed to do it within a much shorter timeframe than usual. Even though I was forced to leave before the full 18 months was up, I can proudly say that I was successful in the time I was there."

The judge studied him for what felt like an eternity before speaking. "Mr. Himes, This court recognizes the progress you made while at Job Corps and your willingness to learn from your mistakes. However, you must understand that actions have consequences."

Jason's stomach churned with anxiety, his entire future hinging on the judge's next words. He couldn't help but wonder if he'd ever escape the cycle of violence and crime that had brought him to this point.

The judge leaned back in his chair, contemplating Jason's words. He appeared to weigh the arguments presented by both sides carefully, and Jason held his breath, his heart pounding in his chest. Finally, the judge spoke.

"Mr. Himes I see that you have made strides while at Job Corps, despite your unfortunate dismissal. You have demonstrated a willingness to learn from your mistakes and make amends," he paused, locking eyes with Jason. "I have decided to dismiss the case against you."

A wave of relief washed over Jason, but it was short-lived. As the courtroom emptied, a couple of teens who had been sitting in the back corner approached him. Their faces were obscured by hoodies, but their hard expressions betrayed their intentions.

"Yo, Jase," one of them sneered. "You'd better watch your back out there. The guys from the hotel ain't forgotten about you. And your own homies probably think you're a coward for bailing on them."

Jason clenched his fists, anger and fear coursing through his veins. He wanted to lash out, to defend himself, but he knew that doing so would only prove the prosecutor's point. Instead, he swallowed his pride, maintaining eye contact with the teen.

"Thanks for the warning," he replied coolly, his voice betraying none of the anxiety he felt. "But I've got my own path now. I'm not going down that road again."

As he walked away from the courthouse, Jason couldn't help but feel that he had just traded one prison for another. While he had managed to avoid jail time, the threat of retaliation from both his former gang and their rivals weighed heavily on his mind.

The streets that had once been familiar territory now seemed fraught with danger. Every shadow held the potential for an ambush; every passing car might contain a vengeful enemy. Jason knew that he couldn't let his guard down for a moment, but he was determined to forge ahead and create a better life for himself.

The sun had already begun to set as Jason stepped into the fast food restaurant, wincing at the smell of grease and sweat that permeated the air. He straightened his uniform, a baggy polyester ensemble that did little to hide his wiry frame, before making his way towards the counter. Jason was no stranger to starting new jobs, but he still felt some trepidation as he embarked on a fresh career. He had worked hard for years and looked forward to the opportunity.

"Jason, right?" the night manager asked, sizing him up with a skeptical gaze. "You're here for the evening shift."

"Yeah, that's me," Jason replied, trying to sound confident, even though he felt anything but.

"Alright then," the manager said, handing him a headset. "Get behind the register. We've got a rush coming in soon, and I need all hands on deck."

As the hours wore on, Jason found himself lost in the rhythm of taking orders, flipping burgers, and wiping down tables. The work was mindless, but it kept him busy—too busy to dwell on the threats that lurked just outside the restaurant's doors.

By the time his break rolled around, his muscles ached and his feet throbbed, but he couldn't deny the satisfaction that came from earning an honest paycheck. He had made it through another day, one step further from his old life.

In the break room, Jason settled onto a rickety plastic chair, his eyes glued to the small TV mounted on the wall. The local news was playing, detailing the latest crime spree that had gripped the city.

"Police have arrested 18-year-old DeMarcus 'Spoon' Johnson for attempted murder," the anchor announced, her voice tinged with fear. "He is believed to be the leader of a notorious gang responsible for multiple acts of violence across the city."

Jason's heart pounded at the mention of Spoon's name. He stared at the screen, unable to tear his gaze away from the familiar face that stared back at him. With Spoon in jail, Ryan in prison, and Nate dead, maybe he had a chance to escape his past after all.

As the news report faded into the background, Jason couldn't help but think about the other members of the gang—the friends he had left behind. He wondered if they thought of him as a traitor for walking away from their twisted sense of loyalty.

"Hey man, you good?" a coworker asked, jolting Jason out of his thoughts.

"Yeah," Jason said, forcing a smile. "Just... thinking."

"About what?"

"Nothing important," Jason lied. He didn't want to burden his new colleagues with the weight of his past. Instead, he focused on the present, on the job that offered him a modicum of stability and safety.

"Alright, then," his coworker replied, seemingly satisfied by his answer. "See you back on the floor."

"See you there," Jason said, standing up with renewed determination. He knew that the road ahead would be difficult, fraught with challenges and setbacks, but he was ready to face them head-on. For now, at least, he had found a refuge from the dangers that haunted him—a place where he could begin to rebuild his life, one burger at a time.

It had been a little over a month since Jason started his gig at the fast food joint. To save money, he shared a small apartment with one of his colleagues. The sun dipped below the horizon, casting a warm glow over the busy street as he made his way home after another long shift. His nights were spent in self-imposed isolation, the flickering blue light of his TV screen providing the only company in his cramped apartment.

"Hey, Jason," called out his neighbor, Mrs. Jackson, as she watered her plants on the balcony. "You're home late again. Everything alright?"

"Hi, Mrs. Jackson," he replied with a half-hearted wave. "Just putting in extra hours at work."

"Good for you," she said, nodding approvingly. "Keep it up, dear."

"Thanks," he muttered before stepping inside and closing the door behind him. He kicked off his shoes, and collapsed onto the couch, letting out a heavy sigh. The TV flickered to life, news reports and sitcoms blending together into background noise as Jason's thoughts wandered back to his old friends.

"Rachel, Consuelo, Calisto… I wonder what they're up to now," he mused aloud, his voice barely audible above the din of the television. "Do they ever think about me?"

"Who are you talking to?" came the sudden voice of his roommate, Mike, who had been hiding in the shadows.

"Jeez, man! You scared me!" Jason exclaimed, his heart pounding.

"Sorry," Mike grinned sheepishly. "I didn't mean to eavesdrop. Friends from your old neighborhood?"

"Something like that," Jason admitted, avoiding eye contact. "I just… I can't help but worry about them, you know? We were really close once."

"Maybe you should try reaching out to them," Mike suggested, grabbing a soda from the fridge. "See if they're doing alright."

"Maybe," Jason hesitated, rubbing the back of his neck. "But I don't know if they'd want to hear from me. I left them behind when I got out of that gang… They might think I betrayed them or something."

"Look, man," Mike said, sitting down on the couch next to him. "You made the right choice. You're building a better life for yourself now. If they're really your friends, they'll understand that."

"I hope so," Jason replied, staring blankly at the television screen. The images of happy families and carefree laughter only served to deepen the ache in his chest.

The following morning, Jason stood at the bus stop on his way to work, lost in thought. He remembered the wild nights spent with Rachel, Consuelo, and Calisto: racing through the city streets, tagging up walls, and sharing secrets under the moonlit sky. Those memories felt like a lifetime ago, and he wondered if his friends missed those times as much as he did.

"Hey, uh, Jason? You almost missed the bus," a fellow passenger remarked, snapping him out of his reverie.

"Thanks," Jason mumbled, boarding the crowded vehicle. As it rumbled down the street, he gazed out the window, the cityscape blurring together into a sea of lights and shadows. He couldn't help but feel a gnawing sense of loneliness, even as the world rushed past him at breakneck speed.

"Maybe Mike's right," he whispered to himself, watching the familiar landmarks pass by. "Maybe I should try to reach out to them..."

As the bus pulled away, leaving Jason with the weight of his past and the uncertainty of his future, he knew that he couldn't keep running forever. It was time to face the ghosts that haunted him and find a way to move forward, with or without the friends he left behind.

The late afternoon sun cast long shadows across the quiet street as Jason approached Cynthia's house. It had been their refuge, a place where they could forget about the troubles that haunted them and simply exist in one another's company. He paused at the edge of the driveway, his heart heavy with anticipation. What would he say to her after all this time?

"Here goes nothing," he muttered, taking a deep breath and stepping onto the front walkway.

But as he reached the door, he realized something was off. The windows were dark and the lawn overgrown, as if the house hadn't seen life in months. His hand hovered over the doorbell, but something inside told him it wouldn't ring.

"Hey there," a voice called from next door. "Looking for someone?"

Jason turned to see an elderly woman, her graying hair pulled back into a tight bun, standing on her porch.

"Uh, yeah," Jason stammered, trying to cover his surprise. "Cynthia and her family. Do you know where they moved to?"

"Sorry, dear," the woman shook her head. "They packed up and left without a word. Nobody around here knows what happened to them."

A wave of sadness washed over Jason as he took in the empty shell of a home that once held so many memories. This spot, which had been such an integral part of who he was, now stood vacant and abandoned.

"Thanks anyway," he mumbled, shoving his hands into his pockets and walking away.

As the sense of loss grew heavier, Jason found himself retracing the footsteps of his past. He wandered through the arcade where he used to work, the flashing lights and blaring sounds a stark contrast to the emptiness he felt inside. If only he could catch a glimpse of Calisto's joyful smile or hear Rachel's infectious laughter again.

"Hey, man, you seen Calisto around here?" Jason asked the arcade attendant, a lanky teenager with slicked-back hair.

"Calisto?" The attendant smirked. "Nah, haven't seen her in months."

Undeterred, Jason continued his search at the park where they used to hang out for hours on end. He found himself sitting on their favorite bench, watching as families and couples strolled past, blissfully unaware of the longing that tugged at his heart.

"Calisto... Rachel..." he whispered into the cool evening breeze, hoping that somehow they could hear him.

But no familiar faces greeted him there either, and as the sun dipped below the horizon, Jason stopped by Calisto's and Rachel's homes only to find that like Cynthia and Consuelo, they had vanished without a trace.

"Dammit," he muttered, gripping the steering wheel tightly. "Why'd you all have to disappear?"

As the night closed in around him, Jason realized that he couldn't keep chasing ghosts. It was time for him to accept the fact that the people he had loved and lost were gone, perhaps forever. And although it broke his heart to think that he might never see them again, he knew that he couldn't let the past define his future.

"Wherever you are," he whispered into the darkness, "I hope you're happy and safe."

And with that, he walked away, leaving the memories of his former life behind him, ready to face whatever challenges lay ahead in his journey towards redemption.

The weight of loneliness pressed down on Jason's chest as he sat alone in his small, barely furnished apartment. The walls seemed to close in on him, and the silence was deafening. He replayed memories of laughter, love, and even danger that had once filled his life. Now, those moments felt like a distant dream, one that he was slowly being forced to wake up from.

"Is this really how it all ends?" he wondered, staring blankly at the peeling wallpaper. "Just...nothing?" Jason reflected on the past 18 years of never-ending highs and lows. He had spent his childhood without much connection until he found a family among his gang of friends, but they were wrenched away from him, only for Jason to find love in an unexpected place with Felicia. Unfortunately, their relationship ended, leaving him isolated once again.

His heart ached with the knowledge that he would never see his friends again, and he couldn't help but feel a growing emptiness within him. But as much as it pained him, he knew that looking back would only prolong his suffering. It was time to make peace with the past and find closure in his newfound solitude.

"Goodbye, mi familia," he whispered, tears welling up in his eyes. "I'll never forget you."

Days turned into weeks, and Jason began to settle into his new routine. Though the pain of losing his friends still lingered, he found strength in his determination to build a better future for himself. One evening after work, he stopped by a local convenience store to pick up some groceries.

As he stood in line, clutching a loaf of bread and a case of soda, his heart suddenly skipped a beat. Standing near the entrance were John and Eric, the two brothers from his old neighborhood. Their eyes met, and a flash of recognition sparked in their malicious grins.

"Hey, look who we found," John drawled loudly, drawing the attention of everyone in the store.

"Long time no see, bitch," Eric sneered, cracking his knuckles menacingly. Panic surged through Jason like an electric shock – he knew there was no reasoning with them. His past had caught up with him, and there was no escaping it now.

"Look, guys, I don't want any trouble," Jason stammered, trying to sound brave. "I'm just trying to live my life, just like you."

"Too bad," John spat, advancing towards him. "You should've thought of that before you abandoned us."

Before Jason could react, the brothers lunged at him. Their fists pummeled his face and body with relentless force, leaving him gasping for air. The world around him blurred as pain seared through every nerve, but he couldn't find the strength to fight back.

"Stop!" he cried out, his voice barely a whisper. "Please, just let me be!"

But his pleas fell on deaf ears, and the beating continued until Jason's vision began to fade. With one final blow, he collapsed to the ground, a broken, bloody mess in the convenience store parking lot.

As he lay there, battered and bruised, Jason realized that while he had tried so hard to leave his past behind, it would always be a part of him – a burden he would have to carry for the rest of his life. But even in the face of such adversity, he knew that he couldn't give up. He had come too far to turn back now, and as long as he kept moving forward, there was still hope for a brighter future.

Weeks passed, and the bruises from the encounter with John and Eric slowly faded. Jason spent most of his time in solitude, thinking about the choices he had made and the people he had left behind. As he stared out of his small apartment window, watching the city streets below, he couldn't help but wonder if things could have been different.

"Maybe I should've done more to keep in touch with them," he muttered, running a hand through his brown hair. "But it's too late now."

The memories of his past life haunted him, but he clung to the hope that he could still create a better future for himself. He knew that dwelling on the past wouldn't change anything. It was time to move forward.

"Alright, let's do this," Jason said, giving himself a pep talk as he got ready for work at the fast-food joint. The job wasn't glamorous, but it provided a steady paycheck and kept him away from the temptations of his old life.

"Hey, Jason!" called out one of his coworkers, Tina, as he walked in. "How are you holding up?"

"Taking it one day at a time," Jason replied with a weak smile. "That's all I can do."

"Keep your head up," Tina encouraged him. "You're doing great."

As the days went by, Jason focused on building a new routine. He woke up early, went to work, and returned home, avoiding any possible run-ins with his former gang members or rivals. It was a lonely existence, but he knew it was necessary for his survival.

"Man, I never thought I'd miss those late-night hangs at the arcade," Jason mused to himself one night as he lay in bed, unable to sleep. "But I guess even bad times can have some good moments."

He found solace in writing, pouring his thoughts and emotions onto paper – his experiences, the friends he had lost, and the dreams he held for a better future. It was a way to release the pain that still lingered within him.

"Maybe someday, someone will read this and understand why I made the choices I did," Jason thought as he scribbled in his notebook. "Maybe it'll help someone else avoid the same path."

Despite the challenges he faced, Jason was determined to make something of himself. He knew it wouldn't be easy, but he was willing to put in the effort to create a life worth living. With each passing day, he grew more resilient, using his past as motivation to push forward.

"Hey, Tina?" Jason asked one day during their lunch break. "Have you ever thought about going back to school or learning a new skill?"

"Sure," she replied, taking a bite of her sandwich. "Why? You thinking of doing something like that?"

"Maybe," Jason said, considering the idea. "I think it's time I start building something more than just surviving."

"Go for it," Tina encouraged him. "You're stronger than you give yourself credit for. Just don't forget where you came from – it's part of who you are."

Jason mulled over Tina's words, considering the changes he had gone through in such a short period of time. He remembered the helplessness he felt while being bullied and the desperation that had led him to join a gang. Now, here he was trying to make something of himself, and it made him question his identity.

What did this make him? Was he the tech-savvy loner who had been targeted for years, or the hardened street thug with a criminal record, or the hopeful romantic looking for his soulmate? It was difficult to say as he was all these things and more. He felt like he lived in two different worlds – one past and one present – but maybe it didn't have to be that way.

The sun dipped below the horizon, casting a warm orange glow across the fast food restaurant where Jason now worked. He stood behind the counter, taking orders with a polite smile, even as his thoughts wandered to the life he had left behind.

"Yo, Jason," called out his roommate and co-worker, snapping him back to reality. "Can you help me restock the napkins?"

"Sure thing, Mike," Jason replied, quickly leaving the register and grabbing a stack of napkin dispensers from the storage room. As he moved through the restaurant, he couldn't help but notice the stark contrast between his present life and the one that seemed like a distant memory. Where once he had been surrounded by gunfire, police sirens, and the chaotic energy of the streets, he now found himself amidst the mundane sounds of sizzling patties, beeping timers, and light laughter from customers.

As he carried out his tasks, he felt a sense of pride in the progress he'd made. He knew that this job wasn't glamorous, but it represented something much more significant – stability, independence, and a chance for growth. His interactions with customers and co-workers were genuine, no longer tainted by the underlying tension that came with being part of a gang.

"Hey, man," Mike said, leaning against the counter next to Jason during a lull in business. "You ever think about what you'd be doing if you weren't here?"

Jason hesitated for a moment before responding, "I don't really like to dwell on the past. I'm just focused on moving forward."

"Fair enough," Mike acknowledged, nodding in approval. "You're definitely different from most people who work here, you know? You've got this... determination."

"Thanks, Mike," Jason replied, touched by the unexpected compliment. He knew that he had come a long way, but hearing it from someone else meant a lot. It was a reminder that his efforts were not in vain, that he could become more than just the product of his past.

"Alright," Mike said, clapping Jason on the shoulder. "Enough deep talk. Let's get back to work before the boss starts yelling."

As they returned to their duties, Jason's thoughts turned once again to his old life. He couldn't deny the loneliness that sometimes crept in, the isolation from those he had once considered family. But he knew that it was a necessary part of his transformation, a sacrifice he had to make in order to build something better.

"Order up!" Jason called, sliding a tray of food across the counter to a waiting customer. With each passing day, he grew stronger and more resilient, proving to himself that he could face the challenges ahead, no matter how uncertain or difficult they may be.

"Thank you," the customer said with a smile, taking the tray and walking away.

Jason returned the smile, finding solace and strength in the knowledge that he was in control of his own destiny. Embracing the certainty of change, he vowed never to let the ghosts of his past define him, but rather to use them as fuel for the fire that burned within – the fire that would guide him towards a brighter future.

The sun dipped below the horizon as Jason walked home from work, his breath visible in the chilly evening air. He moved briskly, eager to get back to the small apartment he now called home. It wasn't much, but it was his – a tangible symbol of the life he was building for himself, free from the violence and chaos that had defined his past.

"Hey, Jason!" A neighbor called out from their doorway as they saw him walking by. "You working late again?"

"Yep, just trying to stay busy," Jason replied with a smile, waving briefly before continuing on his way. As he climbed the stairs to his apartment, he thought about how different his life had become since leaving the gang. No more late nights spent plotting crimes or running from rival gangs. No more living every day with the constant fear of retribution hanging over his head. Instead, he worked hard at his job and dedicated his spare time to self-improvement, reading books and taking online courses to expand his knowledge and skills.

Once inside his apartment, Jason flicked on the light and began preparing a simple dinner for himself. The familiar rhythm of chopping vegetables and heating oil in the pan brought him a sense of comfort and satisfaction. When he sat down to eat, he savored each bite, enjoying the fruits of his labor and the quiet solitude of his own company.

As he ate, Jason's thoughts drifted back to his old friends – the gang members who had once been as close as family to him. He wondered how their lives had turned out and whether any of them had managed to escape the cycle of violence and crime that had ensnared them all. But he knew that dwelling on the past wouldn't change anything. He had made the difficult decision to forge his own path, and now it was up to him to create the life he wanted.

"Whew, long day," he muttered to himself, finishing his meal and standing up to wash the dishes. The sound of running water filled his ears as he scrubbed away the remnants of dinner, lost in his thoughts.

As Jason settled onto the couch with a book in hand, he found solace in the quiet moments like this – moments when he could reflect on his journey and take pride in how far he had come. He realized that the true family he had been searching for all along wasn't tied to any one group of people, but rather was within himself. It was the love and support he gave himself, the belief that he was worthy of a better life, that had sustained him through the darkest days and would continue to guide him on the path ahead.

Closing the book, Jason gazed out the window at the night sky, its vast expanse dotted with stars stretching out before him. He no longer felt confined by the chains of his past, but instead saw endless possibilities for his future – a future where he could build a meaningful life free from the shadows of his former self.

"Tomorrow's a new day," he whispered, determination filling his voice. And with that, he stood up, turned off the lights, and went to bed, ready to face whatever challenges lay ahead, knowing that he was strong enough to overcome them and create the life he truly deserved.

The morning sun spilled into Jason's bedroom, casting a warm glow over the room as he sat up in bed. He rubbed his eyes and let out a deep breath, preparing himself for another day of challenges and growth. As he went through his morning routine, he replayed the previous night's thoughts – about family, self-reliance, and his newfound determination to create a better life.

"Let's do this," he murmured to himself before stepping out the door, ready to face whatever life had in store.

At work, behind the fast-food counter, Jason greeted customers with a smile that reached all the way to his blue eyes. The mundane tasks and routines now held a sense of purpose for him, each moment an opportunity to prove to himself that he could stand on his own two feet, away from the dangerous allure of gang life.

"Hey, Jason!" called out one of his coworkers, Tara, as she stacked trays nearby. "Are you coming to the movie night this Saturday? A bunch of us are getting together at my place."

Jason hesitated, recalling his recent decision to rely on himself for comfort and support. For a moment, the idea of socializing outside of work seemed like a step backward. But then, he realized that part of building a new life was forging new connections – ones not tied to violence, betrayal, or fear.

"Sure, sounds like fun," he replied, offering Tara a genuine smile. "Thanks for inviting me."

"Great! See you there!" She gave him a thumbs-up before returning to her task.

As Jason assembled burgers and handed out orders, he allowed himself to entertain the thought of forming friendships based on shared interests and mutual respect, rather than the bonds born of bloodshed and loyalty to a gang. It was unfamiliar territory for him, but he knew it was a necessary step forward.

Later that day, after finishing his shift, Jason made his way to the nearby park. He watched as families picnicked together, children laughing as they played tag, and couples walking hand-in-hand along the path. It was a scene he had witnessed countless times before, but now it held new meaning – it was a glimpse into the life he sought to create for himself.

"Hey man, you got a light?" asked a stranger, pulling Jason from his thoughts.

"Uh, yeah," Jason replied, fishing through his pockets for a lighter. As he handed it over, he noticed the gang tattoo on the man's arm, and a familiar cold sensation washed over him. His grip on the lighter tightened, and he felt the weight of his past threatening to pull him back in.

"Thanks," the stranger said, lighting his cigarette and handing the lighter back. "You know, we could use someone like you. You seem like you can handle yourself."

Jason hesitated, his mind racing with memories of dark alleys and gunshots, of desperate camaraderie and ruthless ambition. But then, he remembered the promises he had made to himself – to find strength in his own company, to build a life worth living.

"Appreciate the offer," Jason finally replied, his voice steady despite the pounding of his heart. "But I've got my own path to walk now."

The stranger nodded, taking a drag from his cigarette before exhaling a cloud of smoke. "Fair enough. Good luck out there."

"Thanks," Jason said, turning away from the stranger and walking toward home, the weight of his decision settling around him like armor.

As he continued down the path, his thoughts turned to the movie night and the possibility of forging new friendships. He knew that leaving his old life behind would bring its own set of challenges, but with each step forward, he grew more confident in his ability to face them head-on. With determination in his heart and hope guiding his way, Jason embraced the journey that lay ahead.

12

Finding Redemption In Faith

Jason stood in front of his mirror, carefully adjusting the collar of his shirt. It had been a long time since he had felt this nervous about going out with friends, but tonight was different. He had been working at the restaurant for several months now and had started to form a bond with his co-workers. Tara, a cheerful girl who worked as a cashier, had invited him to movie night at her house, along with a few others from work.

"Okay, deep breaths," Jason muttered to himself, trying to calm his racing heart. He ran a hand through his brown hair and gazed into his blue eyes, hoping that he looked at least somewhat presentable. After all, this was just a casual gathering with friends, nothing more, right? But still, there was something about Tara that made him want to impress her.

When Jason arrived at Tara's place, he was greeted by the sound of laughter and the smell of popcorn. He hesitated for a moment before knocking on the door, taking one last deep breath to steady himself.

"Hey! You made it!" Tara beamed, opening the door wide to let him in. "Come on, we're just getting started with the first movie."

"Thanks for inviting me," Jason said, trying to sound confident. Inside, however, he could feel a familiar mixture of excitement and anxiety bubbling up.

As the night progressed, Jason found himself gravitating toward Tara whenever there was a break between movies or someone needed a snack refill. They laughed together at each other's jokes and exchanged knowing glances during particularly ridiculous scenes in the films.

During one such break, they found themselves alone in the kitchen while their friends were in the other room, debating the merits of various horror movie villains.

"So, Jason," Tara began, leaning against the counter and fixing him with an interested gaze, "tell me more about yourself. I know we see each other at work every day, but I feel like I don't really know much about you."

"Uh, well," he stammered, suddenly feeling put on the spot. "Let's see, I just turned nineteen. I've been working at the restaurant for a few months now, and I guess... I don't know, I'm just trying to figure things out, you know? What I want to do with my life and all that."

"Hey, that's totally normal," Tara reassured him, her eyes warm and understanding. "Honestly, I think most of us are still figuring things out. It's kinda nice to have friends who get it, though, right?"

"Yeah, definitely," Jason agreed, his heart swelling with gratitude. As they continued talking, he found himself opening up to her about his past struggles and dreams for the future. He could sense that she was genuinely interested in getting to know him better, and it made him feel special in a way he hadn't experienced before.

As the night wore on and their conversation deepened, Jason couldn't help but notice how easily they seemed to click. There was an undeniable chemistry between them, and he found himself wondering if she felt it too.

"Hey, um," he began hesitantly, his voice suddenly cracking, "do you ever think about... I mean, would you ever consider... going out with someone from work? Like, dating or whatever?"

Tara's eyes widened in surprise, but then she smiled warmly. "You know, Jason... I've been thinking about that a lot lately. And yeah, I think I would be open to it. I mean, look at us – we seem to get along pretty well, right?"

"Right," he grinned, his heart pounding in his chest. Could this really be happening? Was he actually on the verge of starting a relationship with someone as amazing as Tara?

"Let's take it slow, though," she advised, her eyes twinkling with a mixture of excitement and caution. "We don't want to rush into anything or make things awkward at work, right? But yeah... I'd like to see where this goes."

"Me too," Jason agreed, his heart soaring with newfound hope and happiness. Little did he know that this was just the beginning of a journey that would change his life in ways he never could have imagined.

Months had passed since that first conversation between Tara and Jason, and their relationship had only grown stronger. The air was thick with the scent of fresh pine as they stood together on the porch of their new home, far away from the memories that haunted them in their old town. The sun cast long shadows across the lawn, painting a picture of peace and tranquility.

"Wow," Tara said softly, her eyes taking in the surrounding landscape. "I can't believe we actually did it. We've moved away, started a new life together."

Jason glanced at her, his heart swelling with love for this woman who had stood by his side through thick and thin. "It's all thanks to you, Tara. You believed in me when no one else did." He reached over and squeezed her hand gently. "I promise I'll do everything I can to make this new life work for us."

As they settled into their new home, Jason wasted no time in pursuing job opportunities. It wasn't long before he received an offer for a managerial position at a growing distribution company. The morning sun streamed in through the window, casting a warm glow on the letter in his hands. Jason couldn't help but smile as he read the words that confirmed his acceptance.

"Hey!" he called out to Tara, who was in the kitchen making breakfast. "I got the job! I'm going to be a manager!"

"Really? That's amazing, Jason!" she exclaimed, rushing into the living room to hug him. "This is going to be such a great opportunity for us. I knew you could do it!"

"Thanks, Tara," he replied, wrapping his arms around her. "I couldn't have done it without your support."

As the weeks went by, Jason immersed himself in his new role. He proved to be a natural leader, earning the respect of his colleagues and quickly becoming an integral part of the company. The sound of his footsteps echoed through the warehouse as he walked with purpose, overseeing the daily operations and making sure everything ran smoothly.

"Hey, Jason," one of his employees called out to him from across the floor. "We've got a problem with the shipment schedule. Can you take a look?"

"Sure thing, Carl," Jason responded, striding over to assess the situation. He knew that by securing this position, he was not only providing for himself and Tara but also taking on the responsibility of protecting them both from the dangers of their past.

As he worked late into the night, Jason couldn't help but reflect on how far he had come. From a troubled past marked by gang violence and hardship to a promising future filled with love and stability, it seemed almost too good to be true. But he knew that it was all thanks to Tara – her understanding, her faith in him, and her unwavering support.

Jason's phone rang. It was Tara, "It's time to come home and rest. You've been working nonstop."

"Okay," he agreed, shutting down his computer and gathering his things. As he walked to his car, Jason couldn't help but feel grateful for the life they were building together. Away from the darkness of their past, they now had the opportunity to create something beautiful and lasting. And he was determined to make the most of it, for both their sakes.

Through the years, Tara and Jason's love flourished, and they were blessed with four beautiful children. Their home was filled with laughter, warmth, and a sense of safety that neither had experienced in their youth. As their family grew, so did Jason's determination to ensure his children would never endure the hardships he once faced.

"Hey, kids! Who wants pizza for dinner?" Jason called out as he entered their cozy living room, where Tara was helping their one of their sons with his homework, and their daughters played with their toys on the floor.

"Me!" their son, Riley, exclaimed, momentarily distracted from his math problems.

"Pepperoni!" chimed in Leigh, clapping her hands together.

"Alright, pepperoni it is," Jason agreed with a smile, ruffling Leigh's hair affectionately before joining Tara on the couch. "I've been thinking, Tara," he began, his voice tinged with both excitement and seriousness. "I want to do more to help kids who might be headed down the wrong path, like I was. I think I want to go back to school and get a degree in social work."

Tara looked at him thoughtfully, her eyes full of admiration. "That's amazing, Jason. I know you'd be great at it. But are you sure you can manage that while working full time and raising our family?"

"Absolutely," Jason replied confidently, squeezing her hand. "Nothing matters more to me than giving back and making a difference, especially for kids who don't have the support I was lucky enough to find in you. And if I can help even one child avoid the mistakes I made, then it will be worth it."

"Then I'll support you every step of the way," Tara promised, leaning in to give him a gentle kiss.

After a little over three years since Jason began his studies, he was almost finished with his social work degree. It had been a long journey, filled with late nights studying and early morning classes. But in spite of the challenges, Jason never wavered in his commitment to completing his degree.

Meanwhile, Tara had been right by his side throughout the entire process. She cheered him on when he felt discouraged and helped him find time to study when things got busy at work. Whenever they had family time together, she made sure it was quality time spent focusing on their children and enjoying each other's company.

With only a few classes left to complete, Jason was determined to finish strong. He threw himself into studying every chance he could get and made sure he attended all of his classes.

"Mommy, why does Daddy have to go to school?" Alexis asked one evening as they sat down for dinner.

"Because Daddy wants to learn how to help other kids, sweetheart," Tara explained softly. "He knows that sometimes people need a little extra support to make the right choices in life."

"Like when you helped Daddy?" JJ chimed in, showing he had a deeper understanding of his parents' history than they realized.

"Exactly like that, buddy," Jason said, pride swelling in his chest. "And now, I want to be able to do the same for others."

Finally, after months of hard work, the day arrived for Jason to graduate from college. Tara and the kids were there cheering him on as he walked across the stage to receive his diploma. As he accepted it from the dean, tears of joy streamed down his face; this moment represented much more than just an accomplishment—it signified a new chapter in his life where he could use what he'd learned to help others who needed it most.

That night, the family celebrated with a special dinner out at their favorite restaurant — a fitting end to the long road Jason had traveled over these past few years. As they talked about future plans and shared stories from their journey together so far, one thing was clear: No matter what came next for them individually or as a family unit—their love would remain true and strong forevermore.

Jason sat on the porch swing, the cool evening breeze ruffling his hair as he watched his children play in the front yard. The sun was setting, casting a warm orange glow across their happy faces. He couldn't help but reflect on the incredible journey that had brought him to this moment – a journey that had been fraught with obstacles and challenges, but also one that had ultimately led to redemption and a newfound purpose.

"Hey, babe," Tara said, stepping onto the porch with a glass of lemonade for him. "What's on your mind?"

"Everything we've been through, all the ups and downs," Jason replied, accepting the cold drink gratefully. "It's just amazing to think about how far we've come."

Tara nodded, her eyes welling up with tears. "I'm so proud of you, Jason. You've worked so hard to turn your life around, and it's incredible to see the man you've become."

Jason took a sip of his lemonade and looked back at his children, who were now chasing fireflies in the fading light. He could still remember the darkness that had consumed him in those early days – the anger, the fear, the loneliness that had driven him to seek solace in a gang. But he'd been given a chance to change his path, and he'd taken it wholeheartedly.

"Remember when we first met?" he asked Tara, a smile playing on his lips. "I never thought I could be this happy."

"Neither did I," Tara admitted. "But we took a risk, and it paid off. We built a beautiful family together, and you've not only provided for us, but you've overcome so much to make a real difference in this world."

As Jason looked out at his children, he knew that their love had been the catalyst for his transformation. Every late-night study session, every grueling work shift, every moment of doubt – they'd all been worth it because they had led him to this point. And now, with his degree in social work and a promising career ahead of him, he was determined to use his experiences to help other young people find their way out of the darkness.

"Promise me something," Tara said, taking his hand. "Promise me that we'll never stop fighting for a better life – not just for ourselves, but for everyone who needs a helping hand."

"I promise," Jason whispered, squeezing her fingers gently. "I won't let our struggles be in vain. We're going to make a difference, babe. You and me, together."

Jason often reflected on his past. Through his studies, he developed an understanding of the behavior that drove kids to bully him during his school years. He acknowledged that they were likely responding out of their own insecurity. Jason was able to forgive and move on, but the experience always remained a part of his childhood. By understanding what had made him seek out gang life, he realized it was not only for a sense of belonging but also for a close-knit group of misfits who needed each other as much as Jason needed them. Some people's life paths can be determined by a decisive moment in time. They say that at some point, you'll come to a fork in the road, and your life will change based on which path you choose. For Jason, this was true about that one day in 1993 at the arcade. It was a day that transformed him indefinitely— for better or worse. Yet, he wouldn't alter it for the world.

Throughout the years, Jason searched for what happened to those from his past. He found Calisto online and they exchanged a few messages. She had her share of struggles but was hoping to change them. Jason apologized for whatever drama he had brought into her life, despite his best efforts, which she appreciated. After a few more pleasantries, the conversation ended, and they didn't speak again. The other girls were living their lives, facing difficult situations. Jason chose not to reach out, knowing it wouldn't give him back what he desperately wanted. Cynthia and Consuelo's younger brothers were in and out of trouble with the law as expected. As for Felicia, there was no trace of her; leaving Jason to wonder if she was still alive. He wished that the wisdom he had now was something he possessed back then - maybe he could have saved one of them from their fate. But he couldn't dwell on the past forever. Jason had a job to do, and he was determined to do it well. Apart from his regular job, Jason began working part-time at a local shelter for troubled teens. He felt an instant connection with the adolescents dealing with difficult lives and wanted to provide them with the care he never had. Even though he knew he wasn't capable of saving everyone, he was determined to make an impact in as many of their lives as possible. While sitting on the porch with one of the teenage girls, Jason shared his story with her, hoping it would get her to open up about her past. The girl had been living in the group home for almost a year without anyone taking enough time to truly understand her struggles - until that day when Jason took time out of his schedule to connect with her and enter her world. Through tears, she finally confided in him and explained her life story. This moment of trust was something they both needed. Now, after hearing Jason's advice based on his own experiences, she started to find hope in her future and began to believe she could escape her dark past.

Jason knew that he had found his purpose – not only as a husband and father, but as an advocate for change. For in the end, it was love and understanding that had saved him from a life of chaos, and it was those same qualities that would light the way for others, guiding them towards a brighter future. In 2009, Jason became on ordained minister. Over the next few years, he set out on a new journey of redemption, learning how he can best reach troubled youth and help guide them on a better path. He worked in a group home for young teens and pre-teens who came from broken homes. In these kids, he found stories similar to his. He was able to share his experiences and provide direction to those seeking it. In 2022, Jason launched a new online presence called Kids Corner of Faith, where he could reach thousands of kids across the world, to let them know they are not alone. To teach them about God and the correct way to live life, and to give them the sense of inclusion so many kids in our world are seeking. A safe place to learn and grow, without ridicule or judgement. This journey, which is far from over, has taken many twists and turns to get Jason where he is today. In the end, Jason made it to where he was headed all along, despite the many off-ramps he took. Jason will continue to reach out to troubled kids and youth who are feeling all alone, via his website www.kidscorneroffaith.com, email and chat, social groups and one day hopefully, school assemblies.

www.ingramcontent.com/pod-product-compliance
Lightning Source LLC
Chambersburg PA
CBHW032058020426
42335CB00011B/402